BEING ZILLI

My Autobiography

BEING ZILLI

My Autobiography

Aldo Zilli

JOHN BLAKE

Published by John Blake Publishing Ltd,
3 Bramber Court, 2 Bramber Road,
London W14 9PB, England

www.blake.co.uk

First published in hardback in 2008

ISBN: 978 1 84454 506 3

British Library Cataloguing-in-Publication Data:

A catalogue record for this book is available from the British Library.

Design by www.envydesign.co.uk

Printed and bound in Great Britain by
William Clowes Ltd, Beccles, Suffolk

1 3 5 7 9 10 8 6 4 2

Papers used by John Blake Publishing are natural, recyclable products
made from wood grown in sustainable forests. The manufacturing processes
conform to the environmental regulations of the country of origin.

Every attempt has been made to contact the relevant copyright-holders,
but some were unobtainable. We would be grateful if the appropriate
people could contact us.

Acknowledgements

First of all, I would like to thank Neil Simpson for working wonders with my scribbles and helping with the writing of this book. To all of you – mentioned or not in the pages that follow – thank you for playing a big part in my life, you know who you are. In particular I would like to thank Paul Kirrage, producer of Celebrity Fit Club, for making a big difference in my life and making me look thin on TV, to Anne Marie Leahy of GMTV for giving me the chance to go back to my home region of Abruzzo to film cookery programmes featuring my very favourite recipes, to Fiona, Mary and Alison at Limelight Management for making all my dreams come true, including the dream of writing this book, to the teams at Alfa Romeo, Kellogg's, Thomson Fly and Thomson Cruise and all my other great sponsors, to my accountant Geoff Jarrett, and to my personal assistant Luisa Alves for putting up with me for the past ten years. Finally, I'd like to thank my wonderful wife Nikki for being so supportive and giving me Rocco, the son I always wanted, a little brother to my beautiful daughter Laura, I love you all.

Contents

Introduction: Only Just Beginning

Chapter One: Farmer's Boy   1

Chapter Two: The Italian Kitchen   13

Chapter Three: Tragedy   23

Chapter Four: Chasing Girls   43

Chapter Five: London Bridge   71

Chapter Six: In the Army   89

Chapter Seven: Soho   103

Chapter Eight: My First Restaurant   107

Chapter Nine: Wine Bars and Wild Nights   115

Chapter Ten: Meeting Freddie   123

Chapter Eleven: My Own Room   131

Chapter Twelve: Success   137

Chapter Thirteen: Running Away   143

Chapter Fourteen: Royalty   151

Chapter Fifteen: The Zilli Empire   167

Chapter Sixteen: Going Ginger   181

Chapter Seventeen: Live on TV   189

Chapter Eighteen: Big Business   203

Chapter Nineteen: Nikki   221

Chapter Twenty: New Friends   233

Chapter Twenty-One: New Starts   249

Only Just Beginning

Maybe I'm still just a big kid, but I need to laugh and clown around at least once a day. I need to try to crack a joke or to play the fool just to feel alive. Fortunately, I hardly ever run out of tricks. If I can't say something funny, I can always wear something silly. I've got a wardrobe full of wild clothes for that.

But I also need to make others laugh along with me. I don't want people to come to my restaurants and eat my food in hushed, reverent silence. I want them to relax and enjoy it. I want to see smiles and to hear people having fun. I'm Italian. That's what eating out is like back at home. I've always thought that's what London needs.

That and a bit more sunshine!

I fell in love with London the day I arrived, more than thirty wild years ago. Back then, I was only supposed to stay for two weeks. What I really wanted to do was to go off to chase beautiful blonde women in Scandinavia. But London drew me in. And English women blew me away. Tall, posh, sexy. They were the ultimate challenge for a cocky little Italian boy with big dreams and nothing to lose.

Within days of parking my battered old Fiat 1500 on London Bridge, I was hooked on the city. There was nothing I didn't like about England. Nothing apart from the rain and the bloody awful food, that is. Working in restaurant kitchens back then was torture. And that included all the Italian restaurants. Most of them seemed to have Portuguese chefs and Spanish managers, and they all seemed to serve chicken kiev. The only place to buy olive oil was in a chemist's, so no one bothered. The whole thing was bizarre.

I wanted to change it all.

I remember walking around London late at night looking at all the menus. I was always convinced I could serve better, fresher food. I listened in at all the quiet conversations going on in the cramped and ugly dining rooms. I knew I could make restaurants more fun. I was sure I could create a room that would rock.

How I got my first restaurant is a big part of this book – how I made it come alive, how I risked it, nearly lost it and got it all back. This book is about all the wild and wonderful people I have met along the way. And it's about all the crazy things I've done.

I'm older now. Hopefully, I'm wiser. But I still want to entertain. Being Zilli is what life's all about. I don't think I've ever been very big on acting my age, so there's not a lot of point in starting now.

INTRODUCTION

What I've always wanted to do is have fun. I've never wanted Michelin stars. I want *real* stars. My restaurants and my stories are all about Hollywood royalty, pop royalty, even genuine royalty. And they're about all the loyal regulars and the locals who have become great friends over so many crazy years. My life's been quite a journey and it is only just beginning. There have been a lot of tears and tantrums. And there's been a hell of a lot of laughs. Here goes…

CHAPTER ONE

Farmer's Boy

Six-year-old boys should be thrilled when their dad takes them out for the day at Christmas. Especially if they've spent all year dreaming that he will spend time with them. But I wasn't thrilled. I was crying my eyes out. Dad and I weren't off to see Santa or a pantomime. We weren't going to buy Mum a present or do any fun stuff. We were off to the abattoir. It was my turn to help kill all the family pigs. I ended up hoarse with crying and covered in pigs' blood. Oh, and did I mention it was Christmas?

Life on a poor Italian farm is never going to be a barrel of fun. It's about survival, not enjoyment. And life in a big Italian family isn't always all it's cracked up to be either – especially if you are the forgotten final son who was too young to join in any of his big brothers' games.

I was born on 26 January 1956 to a pair of exhausted, shell-shocked parents. My mother Maria was forty-two and had thought her childbearing days were long gone. My dad Massimo was ten years older. If he had wanted

1

a new child at all, he had wanted another daughter. Instead, he got me, his eighth son, born six years after the last of all the others. One day I would be extra help for his fields, but until then he just saw me as an extra mouth to feed – a noisy one, at that.

The farm my dad rented was lost in the Abruzzo hills on the Adriatic side of Italy. We had snowy peaks above us, thick forests all around and very few near neighbours. But we did have plenty of land and there was nothing we didn't try to grow on it, no single inch we didn't work. I was on the team from the moment I could walk. Every spring we would all help plant out our fields for watermelons while the eagles circled above.

We tended the vines, the fig, almond, cherry and olive trees. We had herb gardens stocked with everything and dominated by rosemary. We grew our own rocket, courgettes, chickpeas, lentils, artichokes and asparagus – you name it. We went truffle hunting and we kids were sent out to pick wild mushrooms and berries. That was the fun stuff. The hard bit was that all year ditches had to be dug or cleared to move the rains around. Old bushes had to be burned off and good soils lugged around by hand.

Nothing ever stopped. And the crops and the fields and the harvests were only the half of it. The animals mattered almost as much. We had pigs, cows, sheep, chickens, rabbits and ducks – which meant at least once a year we also had piglets, calves, lambs, chicks, bunnies and ugly little ducklings. That part of farm life should have been paradise for a little boy of six. I loved to nurse the little lambs and thought newly hatched chicks were the most wonderful creatures in the world. But I also knew that these weren't my pets. Going to the abattoir at Christmas had taught me that. Going to the market with the cows always reminded me.

My brothers would walk the cows to auction once or twice a year. I always cried when I saw the herd being taken away by its new owners. I liked the cows' faces – I used to go out into the stable and talk to my favourites when no one else was looking. It felt as if they were my friends. But they didn't get to hang around. If we weren't eating my favourite animals we were selling them! I was a sensitive little boy and it took me a long time to get over that.

Our farmhouse was big, basic and crowded. Mum, Dad, my sister Giuseppina, my seven brothers and I weren't alone. By the time I was walking, my sister and two of my elder brothers had got married and started families. They all lived with us as well. I shared a room with a whole gang of kids no more than a few years younger than me. Back then, I hadn't realised that I was actually everyone's uncle. If I had thought about it, I could have pulled rank – I might have got a bed to myself instead of having to share.

We had a big wooden table to crowd around at mealtimes. My dad said grace before meals and we ate when he did. If anyone was late to the table, they missed the meal. Nothing was saved. We all moved fast, we ate fast, we talked fast. If you wanted to be noticed, you had a struggle because everyone else was always too busy to pay attention. If you screamed, you really screamed. We all made so much noise it would probably be drowned out.

My brothers love telling the story of the day I was left in the fields as a baby. Everyone had been working on the tomato harvest and I was lying on a rug on the ground. When the sacks were full and ready to be taken back to the barn, I was forgotten. For about six hours, I lay and poached in the afternoon sun. Then I practically froze to death when the moon came up. Mum only noticed I was missing halfway though dinner and the family rushed into the darkness to find me.

'You were pickled as red as any of the tomatoes, Alduccio,' my brothers would laugh.

'If we hadn't found you, the wolves would have carried you away.'

'You might have been eaten by bears, or plucked up by eagles, little Aldo!'

I never really understood why this was such a funny story.

As a boy, my main role was to follow my brothers everywhere, every day. I had to watch and learn from them. If there was ever a job I was big enough to do, then I did it. That meant planting a lot of seeds, feeding a lot of small animals and collecting a lot of eggs. I spent my life outdoors, in the sunshine and the dirt. Looking back, it probably should have been a lot more fun.

One thing I didn't like was the fact that you never get a day off when you live on a farm. You can never just lie in the sun and daydream. You can never just play. Cows need to be milked on weekends, just like in the week. You can't leave the pigs without grain just because it's cold and wet. You can't leave olives or cherries on the tree just because it's burning hot. I could see from my dad and my brothers how hard the work was as well. We didn't have a tractor and when I caught up with my brothers I knew I'd have to do the back-breaking jobs alongside them. No wonder everyone was so tired.

I was thinking about all this one day when Pasquale, one of my older brothers, announced he was going into training for the priesthood. Church is central to Italian village life. It was hugely important to my family, so everyone was intensely proud of Pasquale. They said he had a calling. I think he just wanted a break from working in the fields.

I don't think my dad ever scared me, but he did confuse – and inspire – me. He couldn't read or write, but he ran the best business I have ever seen. There were no figures he couldn't remember. He knew where every lira was spent and where every centesimo of our income would come from. With no pen or paper, he was the best accountant I have ever met.

I remember joining some of my brothers and their friends one hot summer night, sneaking out of the house to eat some of the watermelons from one of our fields. They were so rich, so sweet, so tempting. But somehow my dad knew exactly how many he had been planning to take to the market. He knew some had been stolen and he made us work extra hard when we owned up to what we had done. I learned right from wrong pretty early. And I learned how important the little things were when every season was pretty much a new battle for survival.

After the tomato harvest, for example, we would sit and peel the fruit for days on end. The skins would make soups – rich, warm bowls of vegetables and the rag ends of any meat. The rest of the tomato crop went in sacks, then were boiled in bottles for an hour on top of an open fire before being left to cool to make our passata. Dad would wake up screaming in anger if one of the bottles exploded because it had cooled too fast. We all lived our lives in a desperate fear of waste. 'A lost bottle of tomatoes is a lost meal,' Dad thundered. And he had accounted for every piece of our crops, every one of our animals.

We used every inch of our crowded house to prepare and store our food. In summer, the roof would be laden with capers, tomatoes, salt. A lifetime later, I nearly fainted when I first saw how much London shopkeepers charged for sun-dried tomatoes. And I think I did faint when I saw how much you had to pay for dried capers. It's the same with olive oil. We made our own, a whole tree's crop making a single bottle we could then use or sell depending on our need. If only we'd sold it in West London in the 21st century – we could have bought a bloody tractor with our profits!

In the good years, we also stewed cherries, made grape marmalade, harvested honey from our hives and made every type of cheese from our animals. None of us got to enjoy it much, though. We all knew when the hams, cheeses and other cured and smoked stuff we left in the attic all year was finally ready to be eaten. That was when Dad nailed a plank of wood across the bloody stairway. No one was allowed into this treasure trove without his permission. No one could eat anything without his say so.

Of course, the years weren't all good. They never are on a farm. Bad weather was our one big fear. When the rains went against us, we were screwed. Too little water and we were on our knees after days of digging new irrigation channels and carrying buckets around the farm. Too much rain in the wrong season and the animals would have to be brought in to whatever shelter we could find. Feeding them and mucking them all out indoors was just as hard as carrying all those bleeding buckets. When we had to ration food in a really bad season, life got really tense and Dad grew older in front of our eyes.

But rain or no rain, the Zilli family survived. We scratched away at our rented land and we made it all work. The crops we produced proved that Dad had magic fingers. There was nothing he couldn't grow. And he also had a silver tongue – there was nothing he couldn't sell.

I loved to watch him on market days, when all the nearby farmers would set up stall in town. It was typically Italian – a mad, massive, noisy free-for-all. Rules? What rules? There were animals everywhere; traders competing to outbid and out-talk each other. My dad always got what he needed. He had respect because he never relaxed for a single second. It made him a great provider, but a nightmare to live with.

I don't think my parents ever showed each other a single second of affection. Mum was Dad's second wife after the death of his first. But if it had ever been a love match, the passion had soon cooled. I laugh now at the idea that they would ever tell each other that they loved each other. As far as us kids could tell, they hardly even looked at each other, let alone touched. Who knows how they managed to have so many children. With role models like that, no wonder it took me so long to learn about love.

The only time I remember my parents showing any emotion at all was at a village wedding. One of the other farmers asked my mother to dance. Dad flew into a rage, but it wasn't because he was jealous. It was simply that his Italian male pride had been hurt. Back then, marriage was about ownership and making do. What's love got to do with it?

Our whole house was turned upside down for my first day at school. Mum looked at every item of clothing anyone had to find me something clean to wear. It didn't matter if it fitted, and it certainly didn't matter whether it matched. I wasn't being especially hard done by – all my brothers had worn hand-me-downs as well. It's just that Mum had never expected to have another child at 42. So, by the time I came along, there wasn't a lot left to hand down. Anything good had long since been used as rags or to keep the animals warm. I looked like a clown in what was left. No change there then, as my wife Nikki likes to say today.

Despite my ridiculous clothes, I loved school from my very first day.

I was the good boy. I was so happy to be away from all my brothers and to get a break from the farm that I'd have gone seven days a week if possible. It took me nearly an hour to get there every day and the moment I left our gates I felt like a new person. I felt free, as if I could be myself. In the classroom with kids my own age, I noticed how much older my sister and all my brothers were. Despite sharing the house with so many nephews and nieces, I realised I'd been lonely on the farm.

Something else made me rush to school every day. Maybe it was because I hardly ever got any praise at home that I was desperate to get it from my teachers, but

I was a perfect pupil. I was a happy little boy and I would have walked through fire just to hear my teacher say 'Bravo!' for something I had done. I just wish I could have kept that attitude. Right from the start in the village school, I made good friends. We were all country kids and nobody had any money, so no one was judged on anything other than how they behaved. We played with stones and sticks and we loved it.

When I got home most days, Mum would have saved me some of the day's bread, maybe smeared with raw sausage or covered in leftover peppers or cheese. Some of those flavours live with me to this day. When I smell the freshest of tomatoes, I am back in that kitchen, loving my mother and dressed in those ridiculous clothes.

Unfortunately for me, I didn't get to enjoy those calm after-school moments for long. As soon as any of us kids were home, we were supposed to get back out on the land. The circle of life never stopped spinning on our farm. Forget homework. Our job was still to plant, to water, to nurture, to harvest, to store and to start again; to feed and to protect our animals and then to get ready to kill or sell them.

That final bit is why, when I was seven, I started to dread Christmas. Holding the pigs' tails in the abattoir the previous year had been the worst moment of my life. And something told me I'd be doing the same – and more – the following year. I was right.

'Aldo, hold that leg. Don't let it kick you. Hold tighter!' Dad was shouting at me as the first of that year's pigs started to scream.

I had forgotten that pigs could scream. It's the most awful

noise you'll ever hear. They can also struggle like beasts from hell. They knew, somehow, what was going to happen to them. Blood smells. Abattoirs reek. You can't miss it.

It can take up to half a dozen men to hold down a big, strong pig; I was still a boy, but I was supposed to be acting like one of those men. I had the back leg to hold this year. One stage up from the tail, one stage away from the man with the knife. His job is to stab the pig in the neck. If he hits the right vein, the pig dies fast. Over the years, I would find out how often he missed.

Either way, my next job was to hold the bucket and catch as much of the pig's blood as possible. We used that in sanguinaccio, our very own black pudding. Nothing was wasted.

Every Christmas, the pigs were all screaming so much and the abattoir was so crowded that no one could hear me crying. But I always had tears streaking right down my face. Most of me wanted to be strong in front of my dad – I wanted to prove that I was as tough as my brothers were. But part of me just wanted to run away forever. That second Christmas, I remember looking up at my dad when the last of our pigs was quiet. He was just standing there in the doorway, smoking. Always smoking. I don't think he even noticed me. Happy Christmas, Aldo.

Back at home the horrors went on – and I was tortured by the fact that I hated what we were doing but I loved eating the results. It's a confusion over animals and meat and food that has never left me. I'd watch, tears in my eyes, as my dad cut up all the carcasses, again making sure no part of them went to waste. Piece by piece, part by part, we found a use for it all. We got fresh steaks, early on, for the Christmas celebration. For New Year's Eve, we had the trotters, cooked in lentils and herbs. Then the pigs' legs were laid down in salt and dried out in the loft to become cured ham for the following year.

We had sausages, we used the pigs' skin, we hung, dried and cured the meat for up to a year. I knew Dad had to do all this. And like I say, I was happy enough to eat the food it produced. Seeing little suckling pigs cooking on a spit outside the kitchen door broke my tiny heart – but I loved how they tasted. And it's not as if my dad was the only one killing our animals. Mum would kill rabbits with a single blow on the back of their heads. We were all able to hold the ducks' heads between our feet before pulling up their legs and breaking their necks. It was brutal, but it was the way life was.

On Christmas Day, our Italian family tradition was to write notes to our parents, telling them how much we loved them. We put the letters under their plates at lunchtime, then – because neither Mum nor Dad could read – we would read the messages out loud. If it was a beautiful letter – and, of course, it always was, even when I was seven and couldn't write more than a couple of messy words – we got some coins as our thank-you present. Then, between endless church services, we watched Dad go back out into the fields to feed the cows. The farm didn't stop for Christmas. Either that, or maybe he just didn't want to spend too much time with us.

I grew strong, even as a little boy. I was wiry, determined, proud. My new quest was to be noticed, by my dad, my brothers, my teacher, our priest. If one of my brothers, maybe ten years older than me, could carry a bale of hay on his shoulders, then I would drag one along the ground behind me. Suddenly I felt I had to prove I was no weakling. If my brother could milk the cows before dawn, then I had to feed them before going to school.

Even though I was young, I made sure I was part of the gang. The only problem was, I never truly felt it. I never felt I belonged out there with my brothers. Pierluigi, one of my sister's sons, was deaf and dumb and sometimes I felt as if I lived closer to his world. I would listen attentively when Pasquale came home and told us about his days in the seminary. Could that be my world instead?

I'd daydream on my long walks to and from school, hardly noticing any of the parched, beautiful Italian countryside around me. There was somewhere or something else I wanted to be. I knew that from such an early age, I just didn't know where or what it was. One afternoon as I was on my way home from school our dog, Lupo, bit me. Afterwards, I stared at him in shock. I couldn't believe that the only animal in my whole life that we hadn't either eaten or sold would turn on me. I was already sulking that day because my brothers always seemed to be going out dancing and having fun and now I felt the whole world was against me.

Then, one weekend, when everyone headed off for the usual Italian Sunday of church services, I stayed behind with my mother in our kitchen. She had to cook the usual huge family meal for everyone when they returned. I watched her, I helped her, I followed her lead and suddenly my grumpiness disappeared. I was in the heart of the kitchen and I had never been happier. I had finally found my calling.

CHAPTER TWO

The Italian Kitchen

My mother started cooking just after dawn, seven days a week. That's what farmers' wives did. Forget mod cons: we didn't have running water in our house, let alone gas, electricity or heating. We didn't even have a proper oven, just a wood-burning stove in the corner we could hang pots over, with all the ash falling down below. That was where we buried the dishes we wanted to cook. Timings and temperatures you learn by instinct. Nothing is written down, but everything works.

'Alduccio, I need some water.'

I heard that all day every day, so off I went to the well. I had to make a lot of journeys, because I was still pretty young and couldn't manage the biggest buckets. But I was always happy to go, because my mother's tired eyes always smiled when I got back. She always said, 'Grazie, Alduccio,' when I completed my task. Thank you, little Aldo. It was like being in school and I loved it. I've

13

always loved being praised. It's what I had missed out in the fields.

I watched Mum make our own butter and cheese. She would stir, and churn and sift it all out. She made our own pasta as well, using flour from the big sacks of '00 flour' we bought cheaply at the market and stored in the barn. Today I laugh that this kind of flour is so trendy and expensive, just like our capers and sun-dried tomatoes. Back then, it was what the peasants ate.

Making fresh pasta was the foundation of everything we did. Our only tools were a rolling pin and a knife. We created everything. All the different lasagnes, raviolis, pancakes, gnocchis and filled pastas. All the flavour and the flours brought out by our homemade olive oil and the herbs we dried out up in the attic.

Mum was the most creative and inventive of cooks. She was also the most instinctive. Yes, there were the old recipes passed down by word of mouth that she used every week. But she was never able to stick too closely to them. We ate what we had. She had to make do with what she could find. It meant that the challenge almost every day was to work out what could take the place of the ingredients we lacked. We needed to work out which flavours would mask the changes or bring out the proper taste of the additions. It's a skill I don't think you can learn from books or in any expensive degree course. It's what you learn at your mother's knee.

It helped enormously that we grew so many of our own ingredients. I don't think you can fully know food until you have grown it. Today, friends in cities who have allotments back me up on this: just one fresh ingredient that's been grown by hand can lift a whole dish. But you won't know that till you try it. I learned other crucial lessons in our basic farm kitchen as well. Because we didn't have a refrigerator, everything had to be used fast or stored very carefully. Watching my mother do all that taught me enough to cope with some of the truly dreadful fridges I found in my first few London restaurants – and it probably helped save plenty of people from some very nasty food bugs too.

Mamma also taught me the benefit of cooking slowly. Long, slow-cooked stews and rich, strong soups were a huge part of my childhood. So were the chicken broths with shredded pancakes, the pasta and bean soups and the timballos. We made our own bread every day and our own cheese whenever we needed it.

As the youngest of the family, I was also desperate to see Mum make her puddings. We didn't get them often. But, when we did, they could transport me. Ricotta cheesecakes, cantuccini biscottis, creamy layered pizza cakes, fried sweet raviolis. The lavender brûlée I made years later in Zilli Fish was a reminder of my mother and of the treats she sometimes gave us.

I also loved the mood in the kitchen, the way it felt structured and safe. But it was still a place of mystery. I would watch my mum preparing and cooking and cleaning, day after day. She looked so old and tired and she seemed to be getting shorter all the time. Had she ever been young? Had she ever had daydreams? I wondered if she had ever wanted a different life. If you believe the clichés, Italian families are supposed to be big, noisy, loving and open. Mine wasn't. I loved my mum and I felt that she loved me. But we didn't talk about how we felt. I couldn't ask questions about the past.

All we talked about was food. She talked me through every single thing she did, even the simplest tasks like peeling carrots and boiling water. To her, every detail mattered. If you cut corners on a meal, you were effectively wasting the food – and that was the Zilli family's biggest crime. Her lesson was that every ingredient deserved respect. Nothing should ever be thrown away.

'What will we do with this, little Aldo?' she would ask, holding up a bunch of fresh fennel. 'Why do I lay this out so flat?' she questioned, making yet more pasta. 'What do I need now, little one?' she said as the lentils and baby carrots and bright-red peppers went into the soup. I wanted to know all the answers because I wanted my mother's sad eyes to smile when I got it right. I also wanted to annoy my big sister.

Guiseppina and I were always in a state of war. Until my sisters-in-law came along, she was the only girl in the house, and I'm guessing that made her feel special. She must have felt threatened when a new baby arrived six years after all the others. Obviously, I wasn't the only Zilli child who wanted to be centre of attention at all times.

Whenever I got in trouble as a boy, I could bet Guiseppina would appear as if by magic, stirring things, interfering and making it all worse. If she didn't think that Dad or Mum had punished me enough for something then she was always ready to step in and finish the job. As a girl, the one place she had ruled was the kitchen. Now I was in her space the war moved up a few gears. I could see she hated it when Mum taught me something new. She went mad when I could do something she had forgotten. If we hadn't been so terrified of wasting food, we would probably have gone to war over the kitchen table.

As it was, Guiseppina took revenge outside the kitchen. I'm sure it was her who told Dad I had started smoking. He went mad, even though he smoked every minute of the day, just like every other adult I had ever met. But he wasn't angry because I was risking my health. It was because I was hiding in the barn surrounded by hay – I could have wiped out the whole winter's feed.

In fact, Dad seemed to be getting angrier every year. He loved getting into arguments with people from the village. He was always right, even when he was obviously wrong. But, however much he must have driven everyone crazy, he remained popular in the village. He was good-looking and good company. The other farmers and traders were always coming around to visit him – forcing my mum and I to rustle up some good food out of nowhere. And he was always heading out to the village to see them as well.

He always had a moustache, always wore a hat, always looked immaculate. However little money there was, my dad had style. He was Italian through and through. And he had the most traditional views about the sexes. If he wanted to go out for an evening, then he would do so; if my mother wanted to go out, there was trouble. 'You've got kids,' he would say, ending any argument. The idea that he too had kids never occurred to him. He also had a very old-fashioned sense of how men lived. If he wanted something, then he expected it to be given to him right away. Even my eldest brothers had to jump to it when Dad yelled out for something. Behind his back, we would all moan that we weren't sons, we were servants. But no one ever said it to his face.

Then there were the things Dad did not do – things he didn't expect his sons to do either. One of them was cooking. My dad came into the kitchen for three reasons: to get warm in the winter; to get his food all year long; and to complain about the meals, on a near-constant basis.

If he thought anything was wrong with any part of the meal, he would reject or refuse it. No matter that Mum had nothing else to serve or had no other ingredients to use. No matter that she had been up since five and had already fed nearly two dozen people at breakfast and lunch. His dinner had to be perfect as well. Like most traditional Italian men, he was the toughest food critic. My mum was the most creative cook in the world. My dad was Michael Winner. No wonder our standards became so high!

However happy I was in my mum's kitchen, I knew I could hardly stay there every day; I knew my main role was still on the farm. But I started to hold back in the fields. As I grew older, I no longer had the same urge to prove myself as strong or as fearless as the others. I didn't try to match everything that they did – after all, no one had noticed when I'd done so before. It was only at school or in the kitchen that anyone ever said, 'Well done' or 'Thank you.' So that was where I wanted to be.

When I was ten, I was sent on a visit to my brother's seminary to see if I shared his vocation. I was happy to go, because I was desperate for a way to break up the monotony of farm life. Anyway, I liked church. I felt special there when I was part of the services. I liked it when the whole congregation was looking at me. So maybe Pasquale had been right to join up. I breathed in the fresh, new air as Mum and I bounced along the lanes to Assisi in a battered old Fiat 500. It was the farthest I had ever travelled and I was drunk on a weird sense of freedom. I was also in my best clothes, many of which fitted me, and I was supposed to be on my best behaviour.

The seminary was part of a big, ancient set of buildings, all of which were full of serious-looking men in robes and cloaks. It was serious stuff and I knew I mustn't laugh at them. So, of course, I laughed at them. Having been told off, I didn't dare sneak a look at my mum's face when Pasquale celebrated the Mass. I was serving at his side and got to ring the bell. I knew how proud Mamma was. I knew she was crying with happiness and I was feeling a bit guilty about having spoiled her day earlier on.

I held her hand as we said our properly respectful goodbyes and I know she forgave me. I think she had high hopes of seeing two of her sons join the priesthood. But by the time we bounced our way back to the farm, I had decided that this wasn't going to be my life. I'd spotted something strange. There were no girls in my brother's world. I was still very young, but I knew I wanted there to be girls in mine. I would have to find another way to escape the farm.

Maybe education would save me? I was still the golden boy of our village school, desperate to please and lapping up praise and good reports. I loved to read because I could lose myself in stories. I always wanted to be first to read out loud to the class because I loved to perform and make people laugh. I even enjoyed tests, because I was desperate to be named the winner. When I look back, it's amazing I had any friends at all!

Luckily for me, enough of the other kids were happy to put up with my behaviour. None of them laughed because I had started talking about recipes as well as football. And one of them offered something truly magical: his family was one of the first in the village to buy a television. Whole groups of us would squeeze into his house after school to share the experience. It was only black and white, of course, but that was good enough. The programmes weren't even very child-friendly, but that didn't matter either.

I loved spaghetti westerns and we would all sit motionless in the heat watching long Italian films and dreaming about other people in other places. We would act out our favourite scenes for days afterwards. In my mind, I was already a long way away from our hillside in Abruzzo. It's a bad thing to say, but watching television is one of my happiest childhood memories. It is right up there with treading the grapes every autumn and being given warm bread smeared with sausages after school. But I was about to learn that bad times can always burst into the good.

'What's that?'

I sat up straight. We had only been watching television for a few moments when we all heard the screams. My heart was racing. Somehow I knew instinctively that this was about me.

'It's outside.' We all got up and ran to the window.

'It's your mum, Aldo. Look. It's your mum.'

My house was nearly half an hour away. Mum must have been running, and crying, for the whole journey. I'd never heard anything so frightening. I had never wanted to hear my mother cry.

I ran out, followed by my friend and his mother, who started crying herself the way Italian women always do. We're good at grief. But you don't want to find that out as a schoolboy.

'What is it, Mamma? What's wrong? Tell me, Mamma. What's happening?'

'It's Felice.' My eldest brother. The apple of my dad's eye.

'What about him?'

Mum wouldn't speak.

'What's happened to him, Mamma?'

'He's dead, Aldo.'

I was still just ten years old. Everything was about to change.

CHAPTER THREE

Tragedy

'We have to go home, Mamma.' I pulled her towards me and we set off, walking into the twilight. 'It'll be OK, Mamma,' I said, though I knew it wouldn't be. How could Felice be dead? He was my father's first and favourite son. He was handsome, fit and strong. He was the man I had always wanted to be. As my mum and I edged our way down the lanes, I found out what had happened. Felice had been in his car and the police think he had suffered a stroke or a heart attack before crashing into a ditch. No one knew whether the stroke, the heart attack or the ditch had killed him. It didn't matter, of course. We just prayed it had been quick.

Back at the farm, it was chaos. Awful, tearful chaos. English grief might be a quiet, restrained emotion. In Italy, it is noisy, passionate, unrestrained. Everyone was in a hurry, but no one had anything to do. No one sat down for more than a few seconds. Neighbours and friends poured in. My brother Pasquale, the priest, was on his way. I was lost in the middle of all the emotion. I even made peace with my sister.

The whole village was at my brother's funeral. It was bigger than any wedding. When it was over, we tried to go on as before – through it all, the farm had needed to be run, the animals fed and the crops cared for. But losing just one man meant the whole family had changed. It turned out this was just the beginning: more change, and a lot more tragedy, was around all of the next corners.

We all watched my dad give up almost overnight. He was only a tenant farmer, but he had still wanted to pass the farm on to Felice so it would stay in the family. Now he just wanted out. However much help the rest of us offered, Dad couldn't – or wouldn't – cope without his rightful heir. 'No one wants this farm any more,' he would rage at the world. 'No one's here to see it through another winter.' So, without saying a word to anyone, he decided to hand it back to the landlord.

When he did, we were moved down the mountains and near the sea, to Alba Adriatica, near Pescara. Dad wanted to retire and play at being a fisherman. We were still in Abruzzo and our new house wasn't much more than half an hour away from our old farm by car, but, to me, it felt like a million miles. I cried the whole journey. Dad had found a rambling, rundown 200-year-old house costing the equivalent of £2,000. He told my two elder brothers that they had to help pay for it and our family was never the same again.

Pierino and Giacomino had to leave us to earn the

money Dad needed. They headed off to a factory in Switzerland and I couldn't believe how much I missed them. I can't put my hand on my heart and say I had enjoyed much of my childhood. I had been lonely and miserable and out of my depth for so much of it. I'd been too young to see my brothers as friends. But I didn't want to lose them all.

'Come visit us any time, Alduccio,' Pierino said as he and Giacomino left. But I couldn't have put Switzerland on the map. They might as well have been going to the moon.

When those two had gone, we started to rattle around the farmhouse. Life felt like a jigsaw with too many pieces missing. I was eleven and I both wanted and hated change. I was suddenly, morbidly afraid of illness and death. And it was still stalking us.

Pasquale had a heart attack less than six months after we left the farm. We visited him in hospital and because he needed the latest surgery we waved him goodbye in silence as he headed off to Houston, Texas. He was going to be treated by one of the most famous heart doctors in the world, Dr Barnard. It was the first time anyone in the family had been out of Italy, let alone on a plane. The church paid for the trip and the treatment because it looked after its own. When he recovered and arrived home thin and pale after weeks of surgery and recovery, Pasquale said the church had saved his life. It saved my mother's life, as she grieved the death of her eldest son. But it would take something else to save me.

The one bright light in our lives was that Giacomino's wife got pregnant just before he and Pierino left for

Switzerland. I felt as if my mum could get through her grief for Felice and her worry over Pasquale by becoming a grandmother again. But this ended in tragedy as well. Giacomino's wife Pasquina died giving birth to their daughter, Gabriella. It was another noisy, passionate time of grief. Another awful funeral. My brother moved back in with us to help care for his new daughter. He looked as if there was nothing left of him.

This was the downside of the Italian dream. Yes, the idea of so many generations living in each other's pockets and supporting each other sounds fantastic. Yes, it all looks great on TV and in films. But in my reality it was very different. The way I saw it, we weren't always laughing and loving each other. I felt the bad side of it. There always seemed to be someone crying in our house back then. Someone was always ill, someone was always dying. I hated it and I cried so often.

Grief didn't bring my parents any closer together either. Mum hadn't been able to bear living in the farmhouse without Felice and now she was just as unhappy in our new town. She was lost there and she started to close up against the world. Many years would have to go by before our home became the happy house it is today.

Changing school was a disaster for me. I'd been so comfortable with the country kids and I'd never been bothered about how little money my family had. Everyone was equal in the hills. It was totally different on the coast.

For half the year, our new home of Alba Adriatica was

a tourist town. We had a huge bay and wide sandy beaches. By the late 1960s, it had a well-established set of hotels and guesthouses. Tourists came from the big Italian cities like Rome and Milan, but also from Switzerland, Germany and France. It meant everyone seemed richer and much more sophisticated. Even the kids my age were aware of the wider world. Everyone seemed to have more cash and better clothes.

Suddenly I noticed that I looked and dressed like a clown. I wasn't in the in-crowd and that mattered to me. When you arrive somewhere in the middle of a school year, it is even harder to make friends. Every time I walked into the classroom, I felt as if I was interrupting a private party. I felt younger than everyone else and for the first time in my life I felt shy. When the teachers asked questions, I never put up my hand. I refused to read out loud. I hated tests. I never got any praise.

In the country, I had loved going home from school. I spent all day looking forward to those first few moments in the kitchen, with the warm snacks my mum would have made with some leftovers from lunch or dinner. In Alba Adriatica, there were no leftovers. Mum hated our new house just as she had come to hate the old one. We had next to no land. There was only one patch of dark, dry earth she could turn into a vegetable patch. But it would take a season to get going and even then it was nowhere near big enough for her to provide for her family. She had to buy food in the markets, with money she was terrified of spending.

In the bright sea light, I could see how old and how tired she looked. If I was a fish out of water in our new town, then so too was my mother. Life on the farm had been hard, but it was the life she had known. This was a new world with new rules.

Mamma still dressed like the farmer's wife she had always been. But the world around her was changing; she was out of date and out of place. Always a tiny woman, she stooped a little more as she walked down Alba Adriatica's paved streets. Still grieving for her son and her daughter-in-law, she threw herself into church life and closed more doors on the world. We hardly ever cooked together any more. I had lost my closest friend.

It took a new arrival to make me feel happy at home again. My brother Giacomino remarried, but couldn't afford to give his new wife a home near the factory in Switzerland, so his new wife Marisa moved in with us. From the start, my dad treated her terribly. Maybe it was because he resented her for replacing his old daughter-in-law. Maybe he was just angry at Giacomino for being so far away – even though it was my father who had sent him out of Italy in the first place. But Dad never wanted Marisa to be near him. When they were in the same room together, he acted as if she was a maid or an intruder.

He couldn't seem to see that Marisa was a desperately kind woman. She had been thrown into a terrible situation herself, living with a troubled family she barely knew. I think her unhappiness gave her an instant connection with me. We were both so miserable that we bonded. She looked after me like a second mother. She washed my clothes, listened to my problems and became a close friend.

We would cook together some days and gradually she would ease my mother out of her shell, help her recover from her grief. Over the years, Marisa would have three children with my brother, three new nephews and nieces for me. She also turned out to be a wonderful cook and a great listener. She would learn so much from my mother and has now kept her recipes alive for future generations. When I go back to Italy today, it is Marisa's cooking I love the most. In fact, I want to draw out her knowledge for a new cookery book I dream of writing.

When you are happier at home, then the rest of your life can fall into place. I was never going to be a teacher's pet on the coast – those days had gone. I no longer cared about learning or passing exams. But, with Marisa's help, I had started to wear better clothes and I gradually built up a strong set of friends.

I had learned the lesson that lots of shy, lonely kids learn: if you laugh and play the fool and act like a joker, then you get noticed. Maybe the other kids are laughing at you, at first. But if you keep going they might start to laugh with you. Then you get to move in from the sidelines. You get included in things.

That's what I did. I was the court jester. I drove my teachers mad because I was so desperate for my classmates to like me. I didn't care if I disrupted everyone's lessons to prove how funny I was. I was probably the worst possible person to have in the school. But I needed to make friends, and that was the only way I could do it. I learned how to be an entertainer. The more I faked feeling confident, the more secure I actually became. It was bad for my academic record. But it's served me well ever since. And it did the trick when I was a sad little country boy feeling like a fish out of water by the sea in Alba Adriatica.

When I got my new friends, I realised it was fantastic to live so close to them. It was great to have other kids just a few minutes away – such a contrast to the way things had been in the country. I soon started to have fun. Most evenings, my new little gang would dream our lives away trudging up and down the beaches, looking for coins the tourists might have dropped during the day. We kicked footballs around and spent hours roaming about on our bikes. I was a teenager and I loved it.

The other big benefit of living by the sea was also becoming clear to me. It was the beaches – or at least the people on them. Alba Adriatica seemed to be full of beautiful girls, and suddenly I was very, very interested in getting to know them. I felt so sorry for my brother the priest as my gang of mates and I sat and watched the ladies go by at weekends. How could he be missing out on all this?

To be fair, if any of these beautiful girls had actually spoken to any of us lads, we would probably have died of shock and embarrassment! We were all talk. We were Italian teenagers, after all.

At fourteen, I acquired another obsession: money. Dad had pretty much retired when he moved to the coast. 'Now it's up to all of you to earn the money,' he said as he headed off to the local bar to play cards one day. But the money didn't exactly pour in and without the land to feed us we struggled. Everything was so much more expensive at the seaside, and we had next to nothing to sell or trade when we were short of cash. Mum and Dad were no longer exhausted by life on the farm, but I knew they had sleepless nights over surviving without it.

The good news was that we had arrived in Alba Adriatica at the perfect time – just before it began to really boom. New hotels and guesthouses were springing up all the time and while I was too young to work in them Dad soon found me another job. The worst one in the world. I carried buckets of water from the sea to refresh the day's catch at the local fish shop. And I helped carry the catch from the boat to the shop when a new load came in.

It meant I was exhausted, dehydrated and stank of fish every night. Worse still, most days I got paid in fish rather than cash. None of that is what you want when you are an insecure teenager desperate to impress your worldlier schoolmates, let alone all the beautiful tourists!

'Can't you give me some money today instead?' I'd beg for hard cash at the end of my shifts.

'Aldo, your mother can use the fish,' I'd be told.

'But my dad can bring her fish.'

'Take her more. She'll thank you for it.'

Funnily enough, she did. Little did I know that my parents had already made sure that the fishmonger would pay me in kind so we would have food on the table every night. And, in another funny sort of way, I did get some benefit from the trade. We had hardly ever eaten fish up on the farm, so I had no taste for it or any real idea how to cook it. It was almost as new to my mum, but with Marisa's help we all learned together.

It was fun. The main catch was sea bass but we also

cooked monkfish, bream, sardines, squid, clams and mussels – and a lot of other creatures we couldn't even identify. We laughed a lot making up names of our own back then, and we didn't have any preconceptions about what kind of flavours worked or how we should cook things. We were adventurous, bold. We had a few disasters, but we made some brilliant meals as well. Looking back, it was all a useful freedom to have.

Back at school, I was still refusing to buckle down. I'd got friends now, so I didn't really need to play the fool in class any more. But I couldn't seem to stop. I liked acting like an idiot. I liked making everyone laugh.

'One day you'll have that smile wiped off your face,' my teachers would say. But I couldn't see it. 'If you don't focus on your schoolwork you'll never get anywhere in life,' they told me. Yeah, right. 'You'll get the fright of your life when you're in the real world,' they threatened.

What they couldn't see was that I was desperate to be in the real world. Earning meant so much more to me than learning. And I wanted to earn a lot more than a pile of fish.

My first real job – for real money – was in a small local hotel. Apparently, I was going to be serving in the restaurant. All I had to do was carry a few dishes around. What could possibly go wrong?

The hotel manager was a fussy little man who was making himself ill with worry. Now he was darting around, giving me instructions in the bar before the lunchtime service began. 'Aldo, your job is to be invisible. You need to be silent. You need to do exactly what you are told. You must serve the ladies before the men. You must smile. You must be polite. You must not make mistakes.'

But I wasn't really listening. I was too busy admiring myself in the mirror behind the bar. I had been given a proper uniform to wear. It was pretty much the first time in my entire life I had worn clothes that matched and fitted me. I loved it. I had a proper white shirt, slick black trousers, a sharp black jacket and a tie. I reckoned I looked the business; I felt as if I had finally arrived.

The reason the hotel manager was so keen to pump me up with instructions was because my first day wasn't an ordinary day. We weren't just expecting the usual scattering of holidaymakers and locals. The mayor was joining us for lunch. And in Italy at the dawn of the 1970s, the mayor was a very big deal indeed.

The man and his party arrived bang on time for lunch, all dressed up in their finery, all looking immaculate, all expecting the most professional service. What they got was me. Oh dear...

'Just take a tray of drinks round, Aldo. Serve the ladies first,' I was reminded.

But I didn't serve anyone. I got to the middle of the room, caught sight of myself in another mirror, preened a bit, stuck out my chest, gave a bit of a pout and promptly dropped the tray.

Vanity was my downfall. We stumbled through the rest of the lunch, trying to ignore the broken glass and the vast wet patch on the carpet. One of the mayor's lady companions almost fell over when she slipped on an ice cube. So my manager was never going to forgive me. I cried and cried that night after getting the sack. I would never, ever do anything so stupid again, I vowed. I would never get the sack again. Famous last words…

My next job was in the next hotel down. I was put in the kitchen, where the owner decided I could do less damage. I reckoned I was the perfect man for the job, because I was convinced that no one in Alba Adriatica was a better cook than me. No one had a finer instinct. No one understood food better than me or could make better meals, I told the owner. It's a shame, then, that all I did was wash dishes.

Getting my first proper pay packet was wonderful. Having to give most of it to my brother was less so. For all the sadness of the past, the big Zilli family survived. In the Italian way, this meant that everyone was always responsible for everyone else. So, when one of us got married, the rest of us had to pitch in to help pay for it. And, in my family, there always seemed to be someone getting married, so it would be a long time before I had any real money of my own. But I couldn't really complain – I was still at school, after all.

'Aldo, I need to speak to you.' The hotel manager had rushed after me as I headed home at the end of a shift.

My heart started to beat fast. I didn't think I'd done anything particularly stupid or wrong that day. But then, you never knew.

'We've got a real problem tonight. Can you help out?'

Phew. I was off the hook

'Sure, what do you need?'

'It's not in the kitchen. We need someone to work on the front desk all night. And it's a big night for us.'

TRAGEDY

Our usual night concierge had just sent a message that he was sick and couldn't do his shift. And just as my first day serving in my previous hotel hadn't been an ordinary day, so my first night working as a concierge wasn't to be an ordinary night. This time it wasn't the mayor making everyone nervous. We had a star guest staying, an Italian singer and actor with the unlikely name of Fred Bongusto. He was performing in the town that night and was due to come back to the hotel sometime after midnight.

'Just let him in, be polite, make sure he has everything he needs and that he knows you are here if there is anything else,' my boss told me. 'This isn't someone we want to annoy. We want him to come back.'

Trouble was, I didn't really share my manager's excitement. This star guest wasn't exactly of my generation. I couldn't see why he was a big deal. And sitting on the front desk from 9pm waiting for him was as boring as hell. The hours passed at a snail's pace. Hardly any other guests came by and, because I hadn't had time to tell any of my friends I was working, I didn't have any other company to help pass the time. I doodled on the reservations pad. I gazed out into the street hoping some pretty woman might walk by. I put my feet on the desk and tried to stop looking at the clock.

And then I fell asleep.

By midnight, I was dead to the world. It didn't matter how hard our star guest banged on the door when he finally turned up after his concert. I'd been brought up sleeping in a crowded farmhouse with loads of us sleeping in the same bed. I could sleep through anything.

And I certainly slept through that. It turned out that Fred had ended up walking through our flowerbeds, forcing open a window and then climbing back into his hotel room. So the next morning I heard the words 'You're fired' again. I didn't even get paid for the shift.

My last day of school came a little earlier than it should have done. I was out playing the fool on my brother's bike when I had an accident. I was supposed to have been showing my friends how good I was at cycling with no hands and my eyes shut. Not a great idea when you are heading towards the sea on a bumpy street with a big bend on it.

I slashed the whole side of my leg and ended up in hospital, where I made a big decision about the rest of my life. I made it when my sister came to visit me and gave me a massive slap for borrowing my brother's bike without his permission. Suddenly I was fed up with my family. If they weren't hitting me, they were ignoring me. Dad was always miserable and I had to give up most of my money so all my brothers could go dancing, start families and enjoy their lives. Plus, I was still stuck in a school I didn't like and was due to take some final exams I knew I would fail. I wanted to get away from all of it. And an escape plan had started to form in my mind.

I left hospital right at the end of term and I never went back to school to take my exams. Instead, I met up with a friend of my brothers called Nino Ripani; he was five years older than me and he was the coolest man in the village. Nino had just got back to the coast after doing his National Service and he was trying to decide what to do with the rest of his life. He played on the same local football team as my closest brother, Guido, and he was easily the biggest goal-scorer in the village. Nino was tall, good-looking and confident. The girls loved him. The men envied him. I wanted to be him. Somehow, we had become friends.

Today, I'm proud to say that our friendship has lasted well over thirty years. We have had a huge number of adventures together in that time. He was the rock that many of my London restaurants were built upon. Signor Zilli on Dean Street wouldn't have been the same without him – just ask any of our regulars.

In 1971, all that was still to come, of course. Nino was just a hero of mine. He worked in and out of some of the same hotels as the rest of us. But he seemed as rootless as me.

'I want to get away from here.'

'We all want to get away from here.'

'Well, I'm going to do it,' I would say as Nino and I wandered up and down the sea front after one of his football games. I was depressed that I was too young and probably too slow to join the team. I fancied myself as a football hero. All Italians do.

'So where are you going to go?'

I looked out over the beach towards the sea.

'Somewhere that no one knows me. I want to be somewhere big. Somewhere I can get rich.'

'We all want that as well, Aldo. Won't you miss the girls, though?'

We had stopped, distracted, as a couple of beautiful tourists crossed the road in front of us. I knew Nino could get any girl he wanted. That was another reason I was so keen to hang around him. I wanted to learn his secrets.

'The girls here just ignore me,' I said, trying to save face. I had my eye on the daughter of one of the local hotel owners. I'd been following her around like a puppy for months, watching her drink coffee in her dad's bar and trying to talk to her at the local Sunday-afternoon dances we all went to. I might as well have been invisible.

'You think they'll be better somewhere else?'

I thought about it for a long time. 'I think *I'll* be better somewhere else,' I said, finally. It was the most grown-up thought I had ever had.

A couple of days later, I was hanging out with Nino in one of the cafés by the beach. As usual, he was surrounded by girls and I was being totally ignored. 'Is it just because he's older than me?' I asked myself. 'Will I ever get a girlfriend of my own?'

One particular girl was sitting closest to Nino that afternoon. She was German, and she had blonde hair, a body like a gymnast and a really rich, throaty laugh. I knew she was ridiculously far out of my league. But I loved to watch her.

Luckily for me, Nino had started to give me a few tips about chasing women. One of them had been to listen to what they say and not to just talk about yourself. 'It surprises them if you listen. They like it,' he said. So I started to listen to his latest conquest. I'm very glad I did.

'I'm going home next week,' she was telling him. 'There's loads of hotel and restaurant work all over

Germany and it pays really well. You'll get a room and all your meals paid if you get the right hotel. You should come over and work a season there.'

I caught Nino's eye as she spoke. I wondered if he could read my mind. It turned out that he could. Nino knew another Italian guy who was living and working in Munich. The friend had said he was always ready to look after new arrivals and help them find their feet in the city. Nino told his teammates at football that they would have to find a new goal-scorer. He was heading north.

'Do you really want to go too?' he asked me a couple of days later.

I nodded. I really wanted to go. But I was already worried that I wouldn't be allowed. I was still just sixteen and I needed my parents to give their permission for me to leave the country. It took a lot of persuading. Mum was desperately unhappy. I was her baby boy and she was going to fight to keep me at her side. Because we were buying food rather than growing it now, she had been forced to get a job in one of the local hotels. So she asked her fellow workers and tried to find me a million jobs that I could take rather than leaving town. She told me how important it was that I went back to school the following term. She said I should get some sort of professional qualification at college, though there was no way we could have afforded the fees.

By now, Guido was working in a factory making leather bags in the town, and Mum tried to force me to work there. But it turned out I was allergic to the dust. I've never been so happy to be given a medical diagnosis! Mum, on the other hand, was at her wits' end.

Dad was just as negative, though I think that was because he was long past being enthusiastic about anything. To be fair, as parents, they were also genuinely worried about me going abroad. Apart from Pasquale's trip to the hospital in Texas, no one had ever been as far away before. In the end, Nino's influence carried a lot of weight. The whole village knew him and Guido reminded my mum and dad how mature and responsible he was. 'He'll watch out for Aldo,' he told them.

My other brother Pasquale made the last, vital bit of difference. I think he recognised something in me, some desire to escape. He knew I wouldn't find freedom in the church. And he thought that if I was going to go looking for it further afield, I might as well have someone like Nino at my side. He persuaded my dad to sign the consent form – though, as Dad still couldn't read or write, all he did was mark the papers with a cross.

I was heading off on the biggest adventure of my life. I was wearing my best clothes – which, to be honest, meant I was wearing some of my various brothers' best clothes from three or five years ago. 'If nothing else on this trip, I want to stop wearing hand-me-downs,' I told myself. In my pocket, I had something else – some money my mother had given me the night before.

'It's from your father's cupboard. He doesn't know I've taken it.'

'I can't keep that, Mamma. He'll kill you if he finds out.'

'You need it more than he does. I want you to have enough to come home if you need to. Don't worry about me. Just send me the money back when you get a job and no one will ever know.'

I could see tears in her eyes, yet again, as I promised to return the cash. I could also see fear. I couldn't bring myself to think what my dad would do if he discovered the money was missing.

The next day at the little station on the far side of the town, I couldn't stop shaking. I'd never been on a train platform before, let alone on a train. The whole family had come to wave me off – even my sister, who I am sure was glad to see the back of me. My mum, of course, was crying. Dad was smoking. Nothing changed. Nino and I each had a battered old suitcase, which we put in the racks above our heads.

The train was hot and crowded with holidaymakers who were on their way home. We were heading north and would change in Milan before crossing the border into Switzerland around midnight. Then we had an equally complicated set of connections to make before we reached Munich around twenty-four hours later. I couldn't meet Nino's eyes. Did he know how scared I was?

CHAPTER FOUR

Chasing Girls

Munich train station was crowded, noisy and frightening. It was the biggest city I had ever seen, the only place I had ever been to that wasn't medieval. I'd stared out at the modern houses and the blocks of flats from the windows as we snaked through the suburbs. 'How many people live here?' I asked Nino. 'How can they possibly find their way around?' In my head another question had struck me. 'What the hell have I done?'

It was early evening and I was about to experience my first ever rush hour. That wasn't something we had ever suffered from in Alba Adriatica. A whole city's worth of angry, harassed commuters were rushing, head down, across every inch of the station concourse. Wherever Nino and I put our bags, we were in the way. I thought that if I lost concentration for a second I could get swept away on to a train to the suburbs.

'Where is he, Nino?'

We were scouring the crowds trying to find Nino's friend. He had promised to meet us. But there was no sign of him. As rush hour passed and the station became quiet, we started to panic. We were in the Hauptbahnhof, we had no German currency and it looked like we were on our own. When the guy did finally show up, he still managed to let us down. He hadn't found us anywhere to stay and disappeared straight after saying hello. Nice one, mate.

Fortunately, Nino tracked down some other Italian kitchen workers, so we had a floor to sleep on for our first few nights in Germany. Then we knew we had to find work. Nino knew a tiny bit of German, but it was mainly phrases he had learned from the German girls he had dated at home. So it wasn't a lot of use when we started job-hunting.

Nino's first job was in a sweet factory, but the money and the conditions were lousy. So, in the end, we did what so many immigrants have to do: we stuck to our own. We asked around among any other Italians and we found a restaurant that agreed to take us on. Nino got a job out front while I was pushed into the corner at the back to wash the dishes and glasses. It was hot, humid and it stank. And it was no place to get rich. I worked the longest shifts but never seemed to have more than a few German coins in my pockets afterwards.

With so little money to spend, Nino and I started to do some bad things. We stole food from the kitchens, smuggling it out in our clothes and bags. I lifted a few more things from some of the fruit and vegetable markets we passed on the way back to our lodgings. I prayed my mum couldn't see me. Or my brother, the priest.

I was so young and so tiny, I felt like some street urchin sometimes. I was desperately thin – I looked like a chopstick – just a sliver of skin, bone and hair that was growing longer all the time. Once more, I felt as if I was invisible a lot of the time. I couldn't work out how people made friends in big cities like this. When Nino got a better-paying job in another part of Munich, I started to feel even more alone. Although it was an Italian restaurant, I didn't make friends easily. Whole days would go by without my speaking a single word to anyone. There was some kind of pecking order and I was clearly at the bottom of it.

Just as I had when I'd left the mountains and joined my new class on the coast, I felt like an outsider. So I decided to tackle the problem the same way. I had made friends at school by acting the fool. Would it work in the kitchen?

It took all my old bravado to try. I had been promoted from washing dishes and glasses in one corner of the kitchen to peeling potatoes in another. I peeled them all day every day and tried to make people laugh by juggling with them, throwing them around and doing everything short of eating them whole. I forced myself to play tricks and tell jokes and get people to talk to me. I was so desperate to get people to like me. But I was still so young and so easy to ignore.

What made it worse was that when my shifts ended I fell apart even more. For some reason, I had a mental block about my way home. Without Nino, I got lost almost every night, sitting on the wrong trains, climbing on to the wrong buses and exhausting myself as I tried to get back on track. Some nights I would cry to myself as I finally headed home. Then I would find myself crying in bed when I arrived. At my lowest point, I started to cry on my way back to the restaurant the following morning as well.

This was supposed to be my big adventure, but I was a lost soul. I had only just turned sixteen and I missed my mum so much. I wanted to go home, but I knew I couldn't until I had earned enough to repay the money Mum had lifted from my dad. And it was so isolating back then. Not only were there no mobile phones, there were no private landlines either. If I had enough coins, I could ring from public call boxes near the restaurant. But I could only ring other public call boxes or friends' houses back in Alba Adriatica, because my mum and dad still didn't have a home phone of their own. And I couldn't even communicate with my mum by letter because she couldn't read.

When I did write letters, I could only say the kind of things I was comfortable with the neighbours reading out to her. And I couldn't feel that her letters to me were any better. She had dictated them to friends, so they came in someone else's handwriting. They never felt like they were words from her heart. Reading them made me feel further away than ever.

So why had I left home? What had I been so desperate to prove? For a long time it seemed very hard to remember. Fortunately, as the months passed I did start to enjoy my new city. Munich hosted the Olympics in 1972 and the city had a huge buzz about it. That's why I'm excited about London in 2012. I learned first-hand how exciting the Olympics can be for young people, even if they have nothing to do with sport. A lot went wrong with the Munich Olympics, but it still made the city come alive. I reckon London will do the same once we stop arguing about it.

My other lesson back then was less positive. I found out that every time you lift yourself up, you risk being slapped right back down. I had been moved from potatoes to pizzas in another so-called promotion, but then I found myself in the middle of a typical restaurant scam. One of the waiters persuaded me to help him make some extra cash. He'd take pizza orders as normal but, instead of writing them down and posting them on dockets for the rest of the kitchen staff to see, he would just call them out to me. He'd serve the pizzas, charge for them and slip the money into his own pockets rather than the restaurant till. And, with no dockets, there was no paper trail. It was hardly the oldest or most sophisticated trick in the restaurant book, just one of the many ways you can boost your wages at your boss's expense. But I didn't want to be part of it.

Nicking some leftovers and lifting some old fruit from a market stall was one thing. Organised theft was another – my brother was a priest, for God's sake. I was far too scared of divine retribution to get involved in this. Unfortunately, I was also a little bit scared of the man with the scam. He was older than me, bigger than me and a lot tougher than me. But, for some reason, I still decided to tell the manager what was going on one day. Fat lot of good it did me. We both got fired and I made a frightening enemy. Another reason to cry on my late-night bus and train journeys home – especially as I was sharing a house with the guy at the time, so I no longer even felt safe when I shut the front door.

Christmas had been the worst time of all. I was too ashamed to head back to Italy with my tail between my legs, even if I could have afforded the train fare. I woke up on my own. Back at home, I knew it would be pandemonium. I could just imagine the whole family getting ready for all those church services. I could see – maybe even smell – the cooking my mother had been doing since before dawn. I wanted to be there helping. In reality, there might have been all the usual rivalries, tensions and family arguments. But I was on my own in Germany. I wanted to be with my mum.

Suddenly, I couldn't remember why I had run away. I couldn't say what I had been running from or what I thought I would find. I was still so lonely. I couldn't understand why I wasn't like my brothers. Why wasn't their life enough for me?

When you're at rock bottom like this, you have to hope that the only way is up. And for me, at last, it was. In the New Year, I vowed to make changes and move on. Thinking about Christmas at home had got me thinking about food. I felt I was wasting my time in a pizza restaurant. I wanted to work in a real kitchen run by a proper chef.

I found myself one right out of central casting. Of all things, it was a French restaurant controlled by an

Italian head chef called Vito. He was Sicilian and he was also a violent, volatile, unpredictable lunatic. He threw knives and pans full of boiling water. He screamed and shouted. He swore like a madman and he lashed out at anything and everything within reach. He was also one of the very best chefs I have ever worked for. I learned a thousand vital lessons from him every single day. I couldn't take my eyes off him.

The passions in this tiny kitchen were made worse, I think, by the fact that Vito's brother also worked in the same restaurant, so some typical sibling rivalry was added to our explosive mix of emotions. But, fortunately, Vito seemed to like me. He would kick the hell out of me every five minutes if I did something wrong (and, of course, every five minutes I did do something wrong) but he would also praise me if I did something right. It was the first time I had been praised since my school in the mountains and I thrived on pleasing him and copying his craft. Just like my friendship with Nino, I liked having an older role model to prove myself to. And, for all the rages and violence, there was a feeling of teamwork in Vito's hot little kitchen. I liked being part of a gang. It felt like a family.

I also thrived on the chance to learn. I was shown how to make rich French Béarnaise sauces, soufflés and crêpe suzettes – all the rich French food I came to hate. I still preferred the simple Italian way of cooking, but I somehow knew it was important to learn more about the French style as well. I couldn't have had a better teacher than Vito. My goal every day was to impress that angry, passionate older man. In the process, my whole experience of Munich changed. It was because of Vito that I was able to survive in the city.

He got me through the three months it took me to save my mum's money and send it back to her. The hope of impressing him gave me a reason to turn up each day. Getting even a grunt of praise made the longest and hottest of shifts feel worth it. I started to stride though the streets to and from the restaurant; I never got lost on my way home again. I had been learning some basic German and I was suddenly confident enough to try it out on people. Mostly they laughed, but I'd never let that stop me before.

As the weather got better, Nino and I started to take advantage of all the extra benefits of Munich – which mainly meant checking out the beautiful women in the parks. We also hit a few beer cellars and clubs, though we probably made a ridiculous pair. The cool and handsome older guy with the young, skinny friend who still looked like a chopstick...

By the time summer had come, we were ready to move on, though. Munich was a hot and sweaty city. Back in Abruzzo, we knew the hotels would be full, the beaches would be crowded and the job market would have picked up. It was time to head back home in triumph. That was the plan, anyway.

'Some success you've made, Alduccio. You're wearing the same trousers you were on the day you left.' That's how my brother burst my bubble the day I got back off the train at Alba Adriatica station.

'You should know,' I thought. 'They were your hand-me-down trousers in the first place.'

But I made myself a promise as we headed back to our house. 'Next time,' I vowed to myself, 'next time I won't just survive when I'm away. I'll make more money than anyone in this tiny town. And yes, I'll one day have the clothes to prove it.'

My mum was so happy to see me that she was crying. Throughout my childhood she always seemed to be crying, now I think about it.

'Did you get the money I sent?' I asked her as soon as I had her to myself.

'Yes. He never noticed it had gone.'

Finally, I could stop worrying about that. We had a huge family meal that first night. It was a proper Italian evening with everyone noisy and loud and putting any old arguments behind them. It felt as if it lasted forty-eight hours. Marisa had helped with the food, of course. I seemed to have more nephews and nieces than ever and even my dad was smiling and on good form. I was happy to be home. Nino and I had been right to think that the coast would be booming.

I spent a few days relaxing and doing nothing at home and then walked right into a job in one of the hotels. I wanted a break from the passion and anger of being in a proper kitchen, so I agreed to work behind the bar and on the reception desk. It looked like being a long hot summer and I didn't want to sweat it out behind a gas stove.

More importantly, I wanted to be on show that year. I had thrown my brother's old trousers away and rushed out to buy a replacement pair. I needed to look good because back then I was a young man on a mission: I wanted to get a girl. Italian families don't talk much about sex – and mine didn't talk about it at all. But Italian boys talk about it incessantly. All my old gang were desperate to hear stories about the wild German girls they imagined I had been chasing.

They told plenty of stories about all the tourist and locals I had been missing while I'd been away. If I could believe any of what they told me (yeah, right!), then I was lagging a long way behind. I had to turn words into actions that summer. I was determined to lose my virginity.

But how?

The first place I tried was at the Sunday-afternoon dance clubs that were still so popular in Italian towns. They were great places. There was no booze, no drugs, just fun music and full-on flirting. The fact that the clubs took place in the afternoon and we all knew our parents were probably sitting in the town square waiting for us to come and join them for dinner at the end kept everything civilised. But, like I say, there were no half-measures on the flirting. Before going to Germany, my chat-up routines had clearly been pretty dire. I don't think any of the local girls ever really noticed I was there. But this summer I was feeling confident. Everyone knew I had been working abroad, so that made me cool. People knew Nino was my friend so that helped as well. I swaggered into the club that first Sunday and waited for the girls to form an orderly queue.

I was still waiting when we were all booted out to rejoin our parents in the square at the end of the dance... Clearly, I needed a new strategy.

For the next few weeks, I tried to chat up any girl I saw. Still they refused to queue up for me. Maybe I should have become a priest after all? My love life couldn't have been any worse. My old friends and I would pace the beaches, just as we had done years ago, though now we were looking for girls, not small change. My hair was at its longest yet, falling right down my back and making me look like a walking carpet. Despite all evidence to the contrary, I was convinced this was what the girls liked. And then, finally, I met one who did.

'You've got the longest hair I've ever seen.'

'Thank you.' Oh, God, I hope she had meant that as a compliment.

'You look like a girl.'

Shit!

'But it's pretty cool.'

Saved!

'Do you want to go for a walk?'

'Sure.'

And that was it. I was quite literally taking my first steps. I wasn't sure if I could breathe. She was from Torino in northern Italy, here on holiday with her family. She was just a little shorter than me, which was perfect. She had rich, dark hair tied behind her head, which made her look sporty and sexy. She had a fantastic tan and a perfect body. Oh, and she was wearing a light-blue bikini.

The one thing I can't write down here is her name – because I am ashamed to say I can't remember it. It's not very gallant, I know. But, when I was walking along the beach with her that day, I had something else on my mind. Two other things, to be exact. Getting my hands on them seemed far more important than focusing on the formalities of our introduction.

'How old are you?' she asked as we turned around and headed back to her towel on the beach.

'How old are you?' I replied, playing for time.

She smiled. 'I'm twenty.'

Shit. I was seventeen. This was a disaster.

'I'm nineteen,' I said, without missing a beat.

'Great,' she said. 'We should meet up later.'

We had ice-creams after she had been to dinner with her family. The sun had gone down, but it was wonderfully warm and Alba Adriatica suddenly felt like the most romantic place in the world. Why had I ever wanted to leave?

'So, were you brought up here?' She was doing all the talking. And Nino had told me you had to ask girls questions so they knew you were interested in them as people. I tried to get back on track.

'Yes, with my family. Where are you from?'

She told me.

'Do you live with your family? Have you got brothers and sisters? When did you leave school? What was your favourite subject? Do you like red wine? Can you see that boat out there? Did I ask if you live with your family?'

I started firing questions at her like it was some kind of quiz night. She hardly got to answer one before I hit her with another. 'Do you like animals? What's your favourite food? Can you swim? Have you ever been to Germany? What's the longest train journey you've ever done? Are you having fun? Do you want another ice-cream?

I couldn't stop myself. It was like I was possessed. I couldn't have acted more like a seventeen-year-old if I'd tried. I am going to become a priest, after all, I decided. I'm signing up first thing tomorrow, I told myself. But somehow I didn't have to. The beautiful, sexy, twenty-year-old girl was happy to put up with me. More than that. She wanted to see me the next day as well.

'We should have a picnic in the country,' she said. 'I want to get away from the crowds down here. We can go in my car.'

I was so excited that I simultaneously found it hard to move and hard to stand still. Not only did I finally seem to have a girlfriend, I finally seemed to have a girlfriend with a car. Life didn't get much better for horny seventeen-year-old boys back then. The next day I called in sick at work and we headed up into the parched, brown hills that gazed out over the Adriatic.

She was driving, I was sitting next to her, again not quite sure if I could breathe. We said we would go for a walk when we parked the Fiat 500 in the shade of a beech tree but we ended up kissing instead. This is a very, very good start, I was thinking. But what should I do with my hands?

My nameless first girlfriend was the first to break the kisses and we headed out into the fields. We'd brought a big beach towel to sit on – hopefully to lie on – as well as the food, which I fully intended to ignore. And I soon got my wish. We were kissing again as soon as we hit the ground and my hands suddenly knew what they ought to be doing and where they should be going. Over her breasts, under her shirt and up inside her skirt. It was then that I got surely the biggest and best surprise of my life. This wonderful girl wasn't wearing any knickers. A twenty-year old girl. With a car. And no underwear. I'd been wrong before. Life really could get better for horny seventeen-year-old boys back then.

I think it took about two seconds for me to pull my trousers down, but while it was obvious that I was ready, willing and able it was probably just as clear that I needed some guidance. Fortunately, my twenty-year-old teacher was happy to oblige. She took temporary control and then I was happy to let instinct take over. It felt unbelievably wonderful. It felt as if nothing could possibly go wrong. I should have known better.

'You in there! Animals! Stop that right now!'

Of all the fields in all of Italy that we could have chosen, we had picked the one with the farmer walking right by it. So I'm seventeen, I'm halfway through losing my virginity and I've got a bloody audience. I decided to carry on regardless: I'd got this far, I was so close, I couldn't stop. Fortunately, my partner was just as keen. She rolled us around so most of our bodies could be hidden by her skirt and we tried to drown out the yells and the jeers from over the hedge.

In my mind, though, I was making love with an ice-skating judge examining my every move. I felt as if any moment he might stop shouting and start holding up numbered cards and scoring me for choreography, interpretation and technical merit. Little wonder, then, that we wrapped things up pretty quickly and my overall performance perhaps left something to be desired. As we headed back to the car, I was jumping on air that I had finally lost my virginity. My girlfriend seemed strangely quiet.

'For a nineteen-year-old, you're pretty crap,' was the verdict she gave me as we headed down the valley to her hotel. But it couldn't take the shine off the moment. By the time I *am* nineteen, I vowed, I would be scoring perfect tens – with or without an audience.

Maybe it was the farmer. Maybe it had been my quick-fire questioning the previous night. Maybe it was just the way it goes. But I didn't see much more of my girlfriend after that. I waved at her, once, as she walked across to the beach with her parents. She gave a quick smile back, but didn't stop to chat. I looked for her after work that day but couldn't find her.

She knew where I worked, but she didn't come by to see me. I couldn't imagine that her family were on holiday here for more than a few weeks. So, when three had gone by, I guessed I would never see her again. It had been my first holiday romance and I'd have liked it to have gone further. But, in terms of my overall plan for the summer, it had been mission accomplished. Finally, I had a real smile on my face. Whatever stories my mates told about their exploits with girls, I knew my story was better. It was true. And it also turned out that I was on a roll that year. Another, much older lady was about to complete my education.

I was working my usual shift in the hotel bar when I saw her. She was a tall, tanned and confident sexy woman from Milan. She dressed well, in light, flowing clothes that danced over her body in the sea breezes. When I first saw her come back from the beach, she had tied a rich-green sarong around her waist. Apart from that, all she was wearing was a black bikini top. A wet black bikini top, because she had just got out of the sea. I nearly fell over.

I knew this lady was on holiday with her husband. But her rich olive eyes met mine as she had coffee with him one morning. They held my gaze for just a second too long. I couldn't take my eyes off her and over the next few days I spotted something very odd and very exciting about the way she and her husband spent their time. It seemed that apart from coffee and meals they didn't want to be together. When she headed to the beach, he would go to their room for a nap. When he went for a swim, she would walk out to the shops. And every time she passed me we would share another long look.

The great thing about working in a hotel is that you can find things out. So I found out when they were leaving and knew just how long I had to make my move. The next time the husband went to lie on the beach and his beautiful wife walked past me towards their room, I decided to follow her.

The bedroom door was wonderfully ajar as I pushed against it. My dark-eyed lady put a finger to her beautiful, glossy lips as I walked in. But I didn't need to be told how important it was to keep the noise down. The first time I'd had sex, there had been an angry farmer on the sidelines. The second time I didn't want an even angrier husband or hotel manager in the wings.

Making love in silence made the whole thing seem more romantic, more naughty, more exciting. I was the young guy from the bar. She was my Mrs Robinson. It couldn't have been more illicit or seductive. I was ridiculously young. But this time I think my performance was at least worthy of a nineteen-year-old. And I had repeat performances whenever her husband went for a swim, went shopping or decided to catch some sun. To him, I apologise. To the fellow hotel guests who so often went without coffee or drinks while their barman was absent, I'm sorry as well. But, oh boy, was that a good summer for me!

For so many years afterwards, the memory of those days would draw me back to hotel work, even though I felt more at home in restaurant kitchens. Working in a hotel was always a great way to meet beautiful, relaxed women with time on their hands. All this and bedrooms waiting to be used. You see the attraction?

When the summer season wound up in Abruzzo, Nino and I got back on the train to Germany, chasing the work and following the money. This time I got a job in my poshest Italian eatery yet: the Eboli Restaurant in a small suburban town called Grunewald. I learned about proper service there and about standards. I learned what customers expected and it was good to finally be working in a place where the food we served lived up to the descriptions on the menus.

Another old school friend from Alba Adriatica was working at the Eboli that winter as well. His name was Gianni and we started off as serious rivals. He had been to catering college and reckoned you needed book-learning to be a real chef. I reckoned you needed instinct and passion and could learn by doing. We had a lot of battles about that when the kitchen doors were closed.

This second long stint away from home was totally different to the first. The tears had gone and I'd stopped getting lost on my way home each night. Some of the cocky bravado I showed at work rubbed off on my private life as well. This time it wasn't all just faked for the crowds. I was starting to feel comfortable in my own skin. I was starting to feel genuinely cool.

I grew my hair even longer. And however ridiculous the fashions – and this was Germany, so they were about as ridiculous as it was possible to be – I decided to follow them. I was earning the best money of my life and I spent a lot of it on clothes. I happily climbed aboard any other bandwagon as well. For some bizarre reason, small dogs were in vogue in Munich that winter, so Nino and I bought a Pekinese at a street market and on our days off we carried him around in a bag to try to attract women. Amazingly enough, it worked.

I pick up languages fast and was able to get even further in German that winter. I think I surprised people by how quickly I learned the fun phrases, the slang and the jargon as well as the verbs and the serious stuff. It meant that the German girls who had intimidated and ignored me that first summer were suddenly within my reach. I liked them. I liked their directness and I even found the accent sexy – though, to be honest, I found most accents sexy when it was a pretty girl doing the talking. But had I been spending time with one pretty girl too many?

That winter I woke up one awful night desperate to pee, but I couldn't do it. When the flow finally began, the pain was incredible. A rush of burning that seemed to run right through me. I don't think I knew a single accurate fact about venereal diseases back then, but I seemed to know instinctively that this was my problem. I didn't know what to do about it, though. And as always happened when I was in any kind of trouble, the same fact kept filling my head: my brother's a bloody priest. What's he going to say if he finds out? How can this be happening to me?

I lasted one day of increasingly painful peeing before I gave in. All Italian men are hypochondriacs and I was convinced I was about to die. I'd wanted to talk to Nino, but as we weren't working together I knew I'd have to wait till the end of our shifts before seeing him. And I was so scared and in so much pain I couldn't last that long. So I had to confess to some of the guys in the kitchens. Some of them I hardly knew, so it wasn't the best introduction in the world. 'My name's Aldo. Nice to meet you. And do you know anything about clap clinics?'

Anyway, after what felt like the world's most excruciatingly embarrassing conversation with one of the waiters, I got the advice I needed. (And when he told the rest of the staff about my problem, they all got plenty to laugh about for the rest of the season.) I looked at my map of Munich and found my way to the hospital he had recommended. The one thing – the only thing – that was making me feel better was the fact that this was happening to me hundreds of miles from home. I just couldn't imagine how I could have coped with this back in Abruzzo. Back there, the local gossips probably staked out the clinics to pass on their sightings to the families and neighbours of the afflicted. But then I got my next big shock. The testing process was like some awful conveyor belt of patients, nurses and doctors. And the whole bloody queue seemed to be made up of Italians. There were no Germans, no Austrians, no one from within a hundred miles of Munich. Just shame-faced, shifty-looking Italians. It was totally bizarre.

After half-expecting my brothers and all my schoolfriends to suddenly join the back of the line, I had my wildly embarrassing consultation and examination. I closed my eyes for an injection and headed out of this medical little Italy as fast as my legs would take me.

I think I looked at girls differently for a while after this wake-up call. I'd felt dirty and disgusting myself. I had to stop myself from thinking they might be dirty and disgusting as well. I had to stop trying to endlessly work out who might have given the infection to me – and if she was on some sort of bizarre quest to lay low every Italian man in Germany. Fortunately, some pain-free pees, a few good nights' sleep and a pack of condoms let me put everything in perspective for the future. But I don't think I'll ever quite forget that conveyor belt of misery at the clinic.

When spring hit Munich the following year, Nino and I had planned to head back south to the boom days of another tourist-filled summer in Alba Adriatica. But by then, we had seen so much beyond our little seaside village and were up for something new. We headed home to brag to our families and friends about how great a time we had had in Germany. Then we headed off to have some fun in the South of France. We wanted to see topless women in St Tropez, beauties by the pool in Cannes, maybe get picked up by a rich heiress in Monaco.

First, though, we would have to earn some money.

Our first stop was Monte Carlo, where we rocked up to the steps of the Hotel de Paris. My hair was in a ponytail, hanging right down to my backside. We'd been sleeping in the car on the way to Monaco and probably didn't smell too good – not least because the car had also been stuffed with sausages, salami and ham preserved in oil that Nino's mum had given us for our journey.

Our wild German clothes didn't seem to match the discreet outfits worn by the hotel guests gliding out towards the casino opposite. But I spoke to the doorman, I found out who I needed to speak to about a job and I made an appointment to see him the following day.

That night, Nino and I did the only thing we could afford to do. Just before midnight, while no one seemed to be paying attention, we slipped back into our parked car and bedded down for another uncomfortable night. Just after dawn, I thought the world had ended. The car was under fire and seemed to be exploding. It was as if we were at war and Nino and I both screamed our way awake.

It turns out that they use power jets to wash the roads early every morning in Monte Carlo. If they don't like the look of the cars they see, they spray them as well.

When the waters cleared, our paintwork was almost as clean as that of all the Rolls-Royces around us. Shame it had so many more dents!

Anyway, I got dressed for my big interview in our newly clean car. I checked my look in one of the hotel mirrors on my way across that most beautiful of lobbies. I reckoned I looked as cool as anything. Then I walked in to see the manager.

'You have to be fucking joking. No way. No fucking way.' That, or the nearest equivalent in French, was what he said the moment I walked into the room. I'd not even had a chance to say 'Bonjour'.

But I persisted. Of course I persisted.

I started out by listing all the different jobs I had had to date – throwing in quite a handful that I hadn't had, for good measure. I made up a series of culinary courses I had attended and passed with flying colours. And quite rightly, he didn't believe a word of it.

'If you've done all that you must be at least thirty-five years old,' he said.

I was still just seventeen.

So Nino and I never got to work at the Hôtel de Paris. But, before we left Monte Carlo, a fellow Italian taught me something really important about how to treat other people – though I don't think this was his intention at the time. We had decided to spend one last night alongside the Rollers and the Bentleys in the hope that the rich heiress we'd been dreaming of might be passing. But after eating all our increasingly smelly rations, we were desperate for food. Late in the evening, when all the restaurants were closing, I went to beg for some leftovers. I thought there might be some fellowship among all the other Italian kitchen workers in the principality. I was wrong.

One of the waiters in a side-street Italian restaurant was cleaning up the last few tables when I did my pitch. He had five old bread rolls on a plate that he was about to lob into the bin. But instead of lobbing them my way, he charged me for them. Five francs for five tired little bread rolls. I don't know the waiter's name, but I'd recognise that bastard's face to this day. I actually felt sick, back in our car that night. Not because of the bad bread or the lack of food, but because I couldn't believe that one man wouldn't help another, even when it wouldn't have cost him a centime to do so.

I think that man might be the reason why I've given so much food and drink away for free in my own life. My only regret is that so much of it has probably gone to those who didn't need it in the first place. But that's a whole other story.

After avoiding the street cleaners on our second morning in Monte Carlo, Nino and I decided to head back east into Italy. San Remo was the next stop on our mini world tour, and this time I wanted a live-in hotel job. I was getting a little bit fed up of sleeping in the passenger seat of a Fiat 1500. But, while I got what I wanted, there was a catch. There always seemed to be a catch, back then.

This time, it was that my room wasn't much bigger than a Fiat 1500 and didn't have a single window. It seemed to be carved out of the middle of the vast hotel building so it was like sleeping in a grave. But I lasted nearly seven months because I vowed not to quit until I had enough money to buy a bigger car of my own when I eventually got back to Abruzzo.

The other big event that summer was that Nino and I both nearly drowned on one of our very rare days off. It was one of the few moments when I'd desperately wanted to be back in my windowless coffin deep within the Laigueglia Hotel. We'd been on the beach, checking out the girls, showing off and generally being Italian. Then we found a pedalo that no one was using and decided to head over to some island we could see on the horizon.

Surely that will get us noticed, we thought, strutting off past the girls like the idiots we were. It was a hot day and after pedalling like our lives depended on it, Nino and I were soon dripping with sweat and ready for a break. We reckoned the best thing to do was to jump into the sea to cool off. Unfortunately, we decided to both jump in at the same time and as we splashed around and had a laugh we saw the pedalo float off in the opposite direction – fast. I was a lousy swimmer back then and both of us panicked. I know now that when you're close to drowning you need to conserve your strength and try to float rather than thrashing around like a maniac. But at seventeen years old I was that thrashing maniac.

I remember seeing the sky, the waves, the sky, the waves. I remember swallowing so much salt water I could have been a whale. I thought about my mother, my family. I probably even thought about all those girls on the beach. I really did think I was going to die.

Next thing I knew, I was on my back on the beach. The girls were all there, crowding around and paying me all the attention I had been hoping for an hour earlier. But I wasn't exactly impressing them. I'd needed the kiss of life and as I gradually calmed down and looked around I could count at least six women whom I desperately hoped had given it to me.

Of course, none of them had done so. One of the other blokes had done it, turning into a *Baywatch* hero and ruining my chances of scoring for weeks. Still, better humiliated than fish food. And I got a long way with my new chat-up line. 'I'm so attractive that even the lifeguards want to kiss me,' I said, about a thousand times. I was living proof that one of the best ways to get women is to make them laugh.

That year, one particular woman would change my life completely. Her name was Eddie and she was visiting her brother, one of our fellow waiters in Munich. Nino and I were planning to go to Sweden because we decided that was where the world's most beautiful women lived. Then we met Eddie.

She was half-English and half-Lebanese, she spoke Italian and she seemed just about perfect. Maybe she was also attractive because she was so enthusiastic about life. She seemed like the bravest girl I had ever met.

'If you're going to Sweden then at least come to London first,' she said. 'After all, I think it's pretty much on the way.'

Who needs a sense of geography when you've got the world's sexiest eyes? Anyway, Nino and I decided we might as well do as she said. London could indeed be on the way to Scandinavia and we reckoned we could spend a couple of weeks there before heading back to the Continent. Unfortunately, for all our long hours in San Remo and Munich, we didn't have quite as much cash as we had hoped. Still, we scraped together around £100 or so and bought a Fiat 1500 from one of our friends.

It seemed all the most important moments in my life to date had taken place in a Fiat 1500. Shame that this one didn't work very well.

Nino and I made it to my brothers' factory in Switzerland without any problems. We spent a few days there and should probably have done a bit of work to earn some extra money. But we were in a hurry to see those blonde Nordic girls, so we left after a couple of days and headed towards the English Channel.

That's when things started to go wrong. We had our first serious breakdown on the motorway in France and we didn't have any money put aside to repair it. Money for emergencies? Are you joking? We'd got our ferry tickets, a bit of cash for food and some cheap lodgings and that was it. I think we were hoping petrol would somehow be handed out for free by the time our tank got empty. Anyway, all the cash we did have went to the French garage after we were towed into the nearest town. We would have to find food and lodgings some other way.

Back on the road the following day, Nino and I got lucky. We picked up a hitchhiker and we did something a bit naughty. We charged him for his journey. 'Pay up or we'll drop you off in the next lay-by,' was our basic message. Fortunately, the guy paid up. So whoever you were, thank you very much. You gave Nino and I just enough money to get into Britain and keep our adventure alive.

CHAPTER FIVE

London Bridge

The white cliffs of Dover blew my mind. I don't think Brits realise just how strong a symbol they are of their country. But to an Italian boy like me, they were part of the legend of Britain, all tied up with the kings and the queens, the castles and the traditions and the cucumber sandwiches. They're what we see pictures of in European schools. And they really did take my breath away on that ferry from France in 1974; they really do cut a line across the coast and mark out the difference between land and sea. They're beautiful.

It was a rough crossing, a world away from the calm waters of the Mediterranean. But that only added to the thrill. Crossing a sea was my biggest journey yet. This really felt like a whole new life. I was going to conquer those big white cliffs. I felt like I could conquer a new world.

Only problem was that Nino and I were nearly killed the moment our Fiat 1500 hit the Dover roads. Nino was behind the wheel, ready to drive us up to London. I'd have read the map, if we'd had one. Or I'd have read the signs, if my English was up to it. As it was, I just tried to keep Nino calm because everyone in England seemed to hate us the moment they saw us.

'Tosser!'

'Get the **** out of here!'

'Wankers!'

'What's the matter with these people?'

Nino and I were hugely frustrated and angry during those first hours. Great Britain didn't seem to want to welcome two happy young Italian immigrants. Cars hooted at us, drivers swore and gesticulated. Even pedestrians tried to rush out and abuse us, anger and aggression written all over their pale English faces.

Germany and France hadn't exactly rolled out a welcome mat for us. But at least they hadn't made such big efforts to send us packing. Like I say, our plan had always been to spend just two weeks in Britain before heading up to Scandinavia. It already felt like we had planned on spending two weeks too long. If this is the stiff upper lip and the English reserve, then you can keep it, we said. Life's too short.

It was when yet another huge lorry tried to run us off the road that it clicked. The driver blocked our way and came thundering out of his cab to yell at us in person. 'Where the hell are you from? You're on the wrong side of the bleeding road!' he shouted. 'We drive on the left in this bleeding country!' So we learned two things: how to stay alive and a new swear word. Not bad for our first morning in country.

Unfortunately for the drivers of Kent, things weren't that much better once our lorry driver had put us right about British roads. Nino took a while to get the positioning right and I was terrified sitting where I thought the driver should be. Every time another car came towards us, I thought I was going to die. Neither of us liked the narrow roads or the volume of traffic we found when we finally reached London, so I pity anyone following our footsteps today, when things are a million times worse.

Anyway, we got into London, made our way through some dreary South London streets as if we were in dodgem cars, found a bridge we could park beside and decided to explore. As it turned out, this wasn't just any old bridge. It was London Bridge. Without a map and without a plan, we had managed to get right to the heart of town. That had to be a good sign.

Unfortunately, we had a very bad sign when we headed back to the bridge after pounding the streets all day. We had clocked most of the key London sights, but we couldn't find the car. It might have been stolen, it might have been towed away. For all I know, it might still be rusting away on some forgotten side street in the City. But Nino and I never saw it again. The blonde Scandinavian girls might have to wait a bit longer for us. It looked like we would need to stay in London for a little longer than planned.

We met up with Eddie, as planned, and because she knew a lot of people we knew a lot of people. That helped us find floors to sleep on for our first few nights and jobs to do in our first few weeks. Meeting people who know people would end up as my way of life. Making friends. Always trying to see how far a few jokes and a bit of fun could take me.

My English was still pretty lousy, so part of me wanted to find other Italians to hang out with. London was easily the biggest city I'd ever seen and I knew it would be easier to cope if I stuck to my fellow countrymen. But I also knew I'd never get to the heart of it that way. I wanted to see as much of the place as possible and to speak to as many people as I could. Nino and I walked so many streets in those first few days – tourist sites, places like Carnaby Street and the King's Road, little alleyways by the river and in Soho. We tried to chat to people everywhere. And everyone amazed us.

British people seemed so confident, so busy, so different. Something told me I wanted to be part of all of this, to jump in with both feet. I decided to allow myself to have Italian friends, but I vowed I would only ever have English girlfriends. If I forced myself to chat up women in English, I would have an incentive to learn fast. And, while people always say they think Italian, Spanish or French accents are sexy, I thought the same about English. I love the language. To me it was mellow, seductive – especially after spending so long in Germany. And in the late 1970s it was still spoken so properly. On television and on the radio, the presenters sounded like something out of a black-and-white movie. It was posh, correct and I loved it.

Over the years, I've also loved the way English people are so brave with their language. I love the jargon, the swear words, the silly little phrases that pop up out of nowhere and seem to be on everyone's lips for a season. All my life I've enjoyed surprising people by throwing those into my conversations. People expect you to speak a very basic English when you're from somewhere else. I love to see people's faces when I try my cockney accent or use the latest words from the street.

After our first few nights of sleeping on floors, Nino and I realised we had to get a bit more serious. Without a car, we had no easy way back to the Continent. We would need to stay a while and earn some cash. We slept at Eddie's for a while but because she and I were dating Nino got jealous and headed off on his own. But she still found us jobs in the Seven Hills Hotel near Epsom in Surrey. They were live-in posts, so we got somewhere free to sleep. We also got free meals. But that turned out to be bad news. Sausage, chips and a glass of milk on Monday. Sausage, chips and a glass of milk on Tuesday. Sausage, chips and a glass of milk on Wednesday. You get the picture. I got hunger pains and stomach cramps.

The other bad thing about life at Seven Hills was that it looked as if I was going to be trapped in the kitchen. That's where the boss wanted to put me. Most of the other kitchen staff were Italians, so I suppose they thought we would all be best off together. But I hated that. I wanted to be out there in the restaurant, working on my English. By then I'd borrowed a set of Linguaphone tapes and was desperate to practise. But when the boss finally gave in to me, I blew it. After only a few days front-of-house, I was serving a flaming crêpe suzette (or at least what passed for one back in 1970s

Britain) and I got a bit too carried away by being theatrical and providing a real sense of occasion to the diners.

Somehow, I missed the fact that the crêpe was edging ever closer to the edge of the plate... It then got its critical momentum and ended up on the very ample chest of a well-dressed woman with one of the posh English accents I was desperate to acquire. Polyester was still in fashion, so she very nearly caught fire as she shrieked and pushed the flaming pancake off her bosoms.

I learned some surprising new words from this woman and her equally posh husband that day. And I learned what the words 'You're fired' sounded like in English when the hotel manager had his say at the end of my shift.

By this point, Eddie and I were pretty serious about each other – we'd been dating pretty much since our first meeting in Munich. I loved everything about her, from her body to her spirit to her accent. And I loved the fact that someone as sophisticated as her was ready to have fun with a poor little country boy like me. We couldn't really have been more different. But we clicked. If only her family had seen it that way!

The first dinner I had with her parents was in what felt like some sort of manor house out in the suburbs. Looking back, it was nowhere near as posh as it seemed at the time, but it was still pretty intimidating. I sat at dinner in no-man's-land in the middle of their table, forgetting all my English and feeling like a farm boy again. Long silences echoed round the room and even when I stared at my plate I had a feeling that Eddie's parents were looking at me in horror. But Eddie and I were not to be parted, whatever her posh parents said.

I reckon her dad, in particular, had two reasons to be horrified. First, his darling daughter hadn't picked a boy from Eton or Harrow and was stepping out with a greasy, ridiculously long-haired Italian. I could tell he wasn't sure how he could explain that at the golf club. Second, I knew he didn't like the fact that the greasy, long-haired Italian was looking for work in a restaurant. It was too much for him.

'Aldo, dear boy, we've been thinking about your future.'

I was back at the family home for another tense afternoon. I looked up, unsure what Eddie's father was saying. Was I about to find myself under a bridge in a sack weighed down with bricks? My Italian roots were showing.

'My future?'

'Yes, your career. We were thinking you are an ideal candidate for something other than the restaurant trade. I think you should try your hand at something more suitable. I've spoken to some people and we can give you a start in stockbroking.'

I'm not sure what I said to that. Could anyone be a less likely stockbroker than me?

Clearly, Eddie's father had decided that if he couldn't change my nationality or my long hair, he could still change my job. Full marks for trying. My first day as a stockbroker was set up for the following week. I was to follow Eddie's uncle to his office in the City, where I would learn the ropes. Apparently, I could join the rest of the old boys and earn thousands of pounds a day.

Then I could give Eddie the kind of lifestyle her father felt she deserved. Oh dear.

For the big day I had borrowed a pin-striped suit, but I was refusing to cut my hair. As usual, I looked like a clown. The office was surreal. Huge, open plan and wild. And I thought kitchens could be high-pressure, violent and angry places. It was like a scene from the film *Wall Street*. The men – and almost all of them were men – twisted themselves up in the cords of endless numbers of telephones.

They shouted and screamed across the office at each other, using codes and gestures that meant nothing to me. I thought the whole world had gone mad. Lunch wasn't yet for wimps, so we took a break in the middle of the day and I don't think I have ever felt so foreign. These braying, horsey, posh men were like none I had ever met before. If they had been the first British people I had ever known, I would have got the ferry straight back to France. And I didn't even particularly like France. Over lunch in some City basement restaurant, I couldn't think of a single thing to say, a single part of the conversation I could join.

Day Two was just as bad. I hated my pin-striped suit. I hated all the other suits on the Tube. And I was literally terrified of the office. I knew I would never get to grips with the jobs they were doing. I didn't care either. I wanted to make money, but only out of something I enjoyed. I couldn't twist myself up in telephones and send semaphore signals to some chinless wonder whose daddy owned Bedfordshire.

I don't think I knew exactly what I did want to do

with my life. But I had found the thing to avoid. And anyway, this was never going to work. I could hardly see rich customers flocking to Zilli Stockbrokers Ltd, Zilli Investment Advice or Zilli Financial Planning. As far as company names go, Zilli Bankers might have caught on if the customers had a sense of humour. But I already wanted out. So Day Three came and went without me. My City career was over. Eddie's uncle and father were not impressed and after a few great years as a couple Eddie and I soon split up. I wanted to get back to the kitchen.

There is an obvious problem with live-in jobs. When you lose one of them, you lose your bed as well as your income. That's what I had found out at the Seven Hills Hotel. And, while I can laugh about my crêpe suzette moment now, I wasn't quite as relaxed about it at the time. I lost confidence easily back then. I was afraid of being rejected and I was still desperate to be liked.

Fortunately, I got lucky straight away. I got a new job and with it I found what I always needed: a new mentor. This one was my head chef, Toni. Like all the other important people in my life back then, he was much older than me. He ruled the Vecchia Roma restaurant in Hampton Court like Henry VIII would have done. Toni didn't chop anyone's head off, but he was such a tough taskmaster I wouldn't have put it past him. However, he was an inspiration to me, one of the very best chefs I have ever worked with – right up there with Vito, the mad Sicilian in Germany. Fortunately, Tony wasn't quite as volatile as Vito – even though I often gave him good cause.

'Cut me some avocados.'

'What's an avocado?'

It's fair to say we didn't have the best start, and he couldn't believe a country boy from Italy didn't know all his fruits and vegetables. But avocados were about the only thing we hadn't grown on our old farm, so I reckon I had an excuse. Anyway, after every mistake or false start, Toni always gave me one more chance to get it right and prove myself. That's what I lived to do.

Toni actually came from near my region back in Abruzzo, so we could talk together in our local dialect sometimes. It created a private world that the other staff couldn't enter. I can't explain how good that made me feel. Toni was the king of his restaurant; I felt like the little prince. I liked it and it was soon clear that he liked me. Years later, Toni told me he had recognised some spark of ambition in me that I'd not even spotted myself. 'I knew you would end up with a restaurant or a set of restaurants of your own, Aldo,' he told me. 'I just didn't know how quickly you would do it.'

In Toni's restaurant I was reminded of formal catering schools and the people who came out of them. I acted cocky as hell and I'd mock all these jumped-up graduates and their book learning. But, of course, I only did that because they intimidated me. I didn't have their proper grounding. I survived by instinct and by watching everyone around me. I realised, quietly, that I would have to watch and learn a lot closer if I was to beat these school-taught rivals. And it turned out that Toni had been right about my hidden ambition. I realised I did want to beat them. I was nineteen years old and I'd been in Britain for less than six months, but I was convinced I had what it took to run a restaurant of my own. Hell, I wanted a whole string of them.

I think it rained every day I worked at Vecchia Roma. I never once saw the sun shine over the Thames or on Hampton Court. I was loving my new life there and I knew I still had a huge amount to learn from Toni. But I also knew that a real summer was about to break back in Italy. And I was still a mummy's boy. I wanted to go home, be looked after and have some fun on the beach.

Alba Adriatica was a breath of warm, ocean air after a winter in England. I moved straight back into my old bedroom – which I finally had to myself – so I could save all the money I earned in the local hotels. That summer, I was determined not to take anything too seriously. 'Jack-the-lad' was one of the great new phrases I had learned from my English friends, and I wanted to become one.

I chatted up women everywhere I went. I hung out with my old friends. I hit the beaches and tried to wake up my pale skin. In the kitchens where I worked, I was an unlikely mix of serious cook and careless idiot. I loved making mischief. Yes, I did want to work and I did want to learn – I knew how important it was to earn money and do a job well. But I still wanted to joke and I somehow knew I could get away with it. If he'd been around then, I think my role model would have been someone like Beckham at his best. Someone who is so talented that he makes everything look easy. Someone who can glide through life, always going upwards, always scoring whenever it matters, always able to pull something out of the hat at the vital moment. That was how I wanted to be.

And for all the disasters and the mistakes, I was never unemployed for long – not ever. If I was booted off a job on a Monday, I won a new one on Tuesday. I had my dad's silver tongue, it seemed. I could talk my way into anything, even if I couldn't always talk my way out of it when things went wrong.

The other great thing about being back in Italy for the summer was that I could hang out in our kitchen at home with my mum and Marisa. After all the awful, heavy sauces of Germany and England, I loved cooking really simple fish dishes again. A bit of lemon juice, a dash of sea salt, a splash of olive oil, some wild rocket and it was done. If you pick your fish well, you don't need much to cook it. You don't even need very long. I couldn't work out why so few restaurants in London hadn't worked this out. But, however relaxed I was on the Adriatic that summer, I always knew I would go back to London. It drew me in a way Munich never had.

The Italian lira didn't go very far in the early 1980s. But on my next few trips to Britain, I at least had a little bit of cash in my pocket, so I started to have a bit more fun. I worked in so many different places over the next few years. Dinner and dance clubs were still going strong and I loved my time at one of the best of them, the Dolomiti out in Sidcup, Kent.

I enjoyed cooking and serving the dinners there. And when I got a break I always danced as well. But, after a while, I decided I didn't want to be out in the suburbs any more. London was the centre of the world. I wanted to be in it. My first home there was a rented room in Clapham for £8 a week. I had to put 50-pence pieces in a meter for electricity. With the shared toilet a long way down a long hall, I soon learned to pee in the dark when I was out of coins.

My room was tiny: a sagging old single bed you could hardly walk around, a huge wardrobe that took up most of the rest of the room and a window that didn't seem to shut properly. I was used to warm ocean breezes. In Clapham, we always seemed to get arctic winds. But, despite all this, I liked bedsitter-land. I'd seen the television show *Rising Damp*, and I was desperate to meet someone as refined and sexy as Miss Jones. Eddie and I had drifted apart. Maybe I just needed someone older and wiser...

As I dreamed about my perfect woman, all those 50-pence pieces in the electricity meter were adding up. I needed work. But London confused me. The clubs and the music and the fashion said it was the coolest and most exciting place on earth. But then I'd see rubbish pile up in the streets and the few British people I had to talk to just moaned about how everything had gone to the dogs – wherever that was.

When I went job hunting, the confusion continued. Lots of places didn't pay a basic wage and you had to rely on tips to survive. There were rumours that waiters actually had to bribe the maître d' with big money to get shifts at some of the posh restaurants where the real money could be made. I didn't know what to do. And when I got a job offer, I didn't know whether to take it.

One part of me always wanted to work in a kitchen, where I knew I could do well. Another part of me wanted to work front-of-house, where I knew I would meet more people and feel in tune with London.

At first, I picked the kitchens. It was a mistake. Job after job, every kitchen I worked in wasn't just tiny, dirty and overwhelmingly hot – they all seemed to be underground too. Food went up in a dumb waiter, dirty dishes came down and I never seemed to see the sun.

'All I want is to see London and I'm living in a bleeding basement,' I'd moan in my ridiculous mock-cockney accent. Not that anyone listened. Everyone else in every kitchen seemed to be drunk, drugged or psychotically angry. So much swearing, so much violence, so many ridiculous fights and battles. There was more drama in the West End kitchens than on the West End stage. Unfortunately, as I worked away in different jobs I also worried that I wasn't really improving my skills. There wasn't any freedom in those first few kitchens. No flair. Not many fridges. All I did was use bad ingredients to make dull food. It was as bad as Munich. And most of all, I was fed up by rich, creamy sauces. Didn't British people know what this kind of stuff was hiding?

In a bid to escape it, I went back south of the river, to where my British adventure had first begun – London Bridge. In my early twenties, I got a job at La Spezia, the classic Italian restaurant buried underneath the arches of the train station. It served cleaner, fresher food and, as I was able to split my time between the kitchen and the dining room, I couldn't have enjoyed myself more.

Me as a little boy (*far right*) with my mother and my two nephews, Felice and Maurizio.

Above: The family!
From left to right: my
brothers Corrado,
Pierino and Mario, my
Mamma, myself, Dad,
my brother Pasquale,
my sister Giuseppina,
and my brothers Guido
and Giacomo.

Below: Me, aged 13. The
trousers were always
too short!

Above: On my 21st birthday with the cake my Mamma had baked me. God knows what my brother Guido was laughing at in the background.

Below left: My brother Pasquale, the priest.

Below right: The ultimate pulling outfits! Nino and me out on the town in the summer season.

Above: My first proper job in the kitchen (I'm second from left). The Eboli restaurant in Munich.

Below: One of my evenings out of the kitchen. Taking orders at the Hotel Splendido.

Above: Move over John Travolta! Clubbing in the South of France.

Right: An army mugshot taken after my arrest and prison sentence.

Above left: David Austin and Andros in fancy dress.

Above right: Me missing my hair…

Above middle left: With Martin and Shirley Kemp.

Above middle right: Peter Straker with Natalie Imbruglia.

Below left: With Terence Trent D'Arby.

Above left: George Michael, clowning around at his own fancy dress party.

Above right: Jonathan Ross at Signor Zilli's anniversary party, looking like the perfect city boy and with the haircut to go with it. Unlike nowadays …

Above middle left: Freddie Mercury with Stephanie Beecham at Peter Straker's birthday party.

Above middle right: With Jon Culshaw, Neil 'Dr' Fox, Bobby Davro and Sharleen Spiteri

Below left: Michelle Collins, with Paul and Stacey Young at a charity event.

Below right: George at Andros's christening party.

With Annie Lennox at her birthday party.

The menu was good, and the front-of-house work helped both my language skills and my bank balance. I saw how important it was for restaurants to have supportive owners and I made some lifelong friends there. We were all young and full of energy. We partied hard. We travelled around the whole city looking at new places and meeting new people. While we couldn't afford to go to many pubs or clubs, we spent a lot of time in bedsit parties and squats. Punk still hadn't really faded and the clothes, the music and the atmosphere were wild; there was passion everywhere. With The Jam, The Boomtown Rats, The Police, The Specials and Ian Dury in the charts, British music was as hard and as cool as it had ever been. It was the best ever time to be in London. And it was a great time to be an Italian in London because the English girls seemed to love us all. I was always happy to hang out with the Italian men from the restaurant. But I was keeping my vow to only date English women. It wasn't hard.

We all found some great Italian clubs near Piccadilly that were always full of – you guessed it – English girls. We got into the old Embassy, the Wag in Soho was brilliant and the Valbonne on Kingley Street was an all-time favourite. It had a tiny swimming pool inside, which seemed the height of cool. I could never believe I was actually there – it was so different to the places I had danced in back at home.

Part of the game for all of us lads was knowing how to get into the clubs. We didn't have much money, so we couldn't bribe anyone. And turning up in groups of two or three guys made all the doormen think twice about lifting the velvet ropes. So I relied on my gift of the gab, my latest English expressions and accents and my attempts at being funny. Getting into clubs is a bit like getting on in life. You use what you've got and you give it everything.

I was always up for challenges like that and the harder it was to break through the barrier, the harder I would work. Being told 'no' didn't ever stop me. It made me keener; it made me want to play the game for longer. And it made everything feel even better once I'd made it.

Back at La Spezia, I was feeling confident about the future. My boss offered me a loan so I could buy a flash new car. I borrowed what felt like a huge £1,100 and bought a bright-red Triumph TR6 convertible. It had big wheels and every added extra going. I thought I was the coolest dude in London and I booked some time off so I could cruise down to Italy in it later in the year. This time, none of my brothers would be able to say I was a failure. Trouble was, I never made the trip. I was about to meet the girl who would become my first wife. For a long time, we would joke that our relationship began with a bang. In truth, it began with a crash: a car crash.

I met Jan at the Valbonne. She was pretty, stylish and very English. Following all the other patterns in my life, she was also a year older than me. She owned a cool car as well. It all seemed to be picture perfect.

'I've just got a Triumph TR6.'

'I've got a Triumph Spitfire.'

'I live in Clapham.'

'I know a good route.'

'Race you there?'

At the end of the night, we set off. We hadn't been drinking – none of us did, because we could only ever afford to get into the clubs, not to actually put any money behind the bar. But I was probably a bit drunk on the excitement of having my new wheels. So when I got to Waterloo Bridge I wasn't paying enough attention to the traffic lights. I thought I had right of way, but so did the mini-cab driver in a battered old Renault 5.

Only after we smashed into each other did I find out that he was right. Worse, I only had third-party, fire and theft insurance so couldn't make a claim. And I had to carry on repaying my boss £20 a week for a car that was now a pile of bright-red scrap. It was more than I paid in rent.

Jan and her Spitfire got home in one piece and despite my embarrassment over the crash we started to date. She was working as a PA and, if she had been hoping to meet an ordinary guy, living a quiet and uneventful life, then she was in for a surprise. The car crash was only the start. My life was about to become more complicated than ever.

CHAPTER SIX

In the Army

When I was growing up, all Italian boys had to do a year of National Service at eighteen. But that seemed to me to be a total waste of a perfectly good year, a year when I could be having a lot more fun doing what young Italian men ought to be doing: chasing women.

I was living in London when my final call-up date approached and I found out there was a loophole in the system. I got my boss at La Spezia to write a letter saying how essential I was to his business. I took it to the Italian Consulate and, amazingly enough, it was accepted. I got a deal that opted me out of the army and still let me come back to Italy every year as long as I never stayed longer than three months at a time. I'm not sure why everyone didn't do that, come to think of it, but there you go.

For a while all was well – and then my mind sort of wandered. The last year that I had gone back to Italy to see my mum and work the summer season, I ended up staying for seven months rather than three. The weather had been great, the money was good and the women were beautiful, so the army somehow slipped my mind. I then headed back to London, blissfully unaware that I had broken the rules. A few weeks after meeting Jan, I headed home for what I told her would be a simple two-week break. It wasn't.

On my first morning back, I had to register with the local police as usual. I borrowed my brother's car to go over to the station and sort out the paperwork. They did their checks, spotted that I had broken my National Service terms and started to get serious. My mum was putting the final touches on a big 'welcome home Aldo' meal at the house. Meanwhile, I was being pushed firmly into a police van. They drove me to the main police station where I was arrested and put in a holding cell in Rome. For nearly a week.

The cell was like nowhere else I had ever been and that first night in prison was like every nightmare I had ever had. First of all, it stank. No fresh air had got in for generations and the remains of every bodily function you can imagine seemed to be visible on the floors, walls, doors and even the ceilings.

The police took the belt off my trousers and the laces out of my shoes. They cut my long, wonderful hair twice in the first three days I spent there. They didn't let me have any contact with the outside world. My cell was so isolated that it felt as if the outside world didn't even exist. And, when I thought of it, I realised my mum would probably be having a heart attack with the worry and the shame I had brought on her.

Five awful days and nights passed before I had a visitor, my brother Pasquale. Priests have a lot of power in Italy and he'd had rules bent just to see me. He promised to bend more to try to get me out.

'How's Mamma?'

I had to ask, even though I could guess the answer.

'She's been crying all day since she heard. She cries all night as well. She can't stop crying.

'Get me out, Pasquale. I'll make it right.'

'Aldo, you're an idiot.'

'I know I am. Just get me out of here.'

But it was two long, bad weeks before even the power of the priest could hold sway. Two weeks when I tried to sleep knowing that the men in the beds around me had killed people. Two weeks when I lost all the dignity, independence and confidence I had ever gained. My task every day was to sweep the prison yard in the heat of the midday sun. It was probably the biggest yard I had ever seen. Just my bloody luck.

I posed for the official mugshots. I was questioned to see if there were other reasons apart from laziness and stupidity that had kept me from National Service. I was prodded and poked by prison doctors in a way that made my spell at the Munich clap clinic seem like a spa weekend. And, of course, what made it worse was the fact that it was all my own bloody fault.

Getting released wasn't the end of the nightmare. I'd had two weeks of hell in prison for missing my year's National Service. Now they were going to make me do that as well. I was handed a uniform, given yet another bloody haircut, and put on a train to the army barracks in Como, up north near the Swiss border. I had no money at all and I was totally alone, unlike all the eighteen-year-olds who had signed up with their mates.

Yet again, I felt like a new kid in a world that had sorted itself out. The other squaddies had had plenty of time to make friends before my belated arrival. And it was clear I wasn't a kid any more. Only a few years of age separated me from the rest of the recruits, but it could have been thirty. I was the old git they wanted to take the piss out of and gang up against. And I couldn't have made it easier for them.

One morning, when they were feeling bored and mischievous, they woke me with some exciting news: 'Aldo, it's OK, there's been a telegram and you're free to leave.'

I snapped awake with a start.

'They say you've got to get over to headquarters now and you'll be released, you lucky bastard.'

'You're kidding me.'

'No. They just sent over the message. You've got to go now, Aldo.'

Why I fell for it, I don't know. But I did. I leaped out of bed, pulled on my full uniform and ran out of the door before I saw how much they were laughing. The old git was an old fool now. Aldo-baiting was suddenly the hottest sport in the barracks.

It was the toughest place I had ever been. But, fortunately, over my first few months of National Service a few things did conspire to turn things around for me. Firstly, I actually found myself thriving on the tasks we were given as soldiers. We learned how to shoot, how to jump off lorries and out of buildings. We were trained how to handle artillery and repair vehicles. It was hot and high in the mountains around Como and the training regimes were endless. But I was a fit old git and a tough old fool so I wasn't going to be bettered by any of the teenagers around me. And I thrived on the challenge of beating them. 'Aldo, you should have done this years ago,' I told myself when I was trying to make myself go the extra mile. 'It would have saved a hell of a lot of heartache. Now speed up and beat those teenage bastards ahead of you.'

The next positive development was that I started to make friends. It was rare for me to get on well with people younger than me, but some of the guys I met that year in the Como and Verona barracks turned out to be some of the best I've ever met. I know many of them to this day and I've respected army life ever since.

But for all the challenges and the friendships, I was hardly cut out for army life. One of the very worst things in my National Service career was the food we ate. It was total crap. And, unfortunately, it was me who was cooking it.

The top brass knew I'd been working in hotels and restaurants, so I was allocated the role of shopping for food and cooking the barrack's rations. It wasn't easy with too little money and too many men to feed, but then I realised that this is what my mother had been doing all her life. I realised I had learned plenty of ways to be inventive with even the most basic of ingredients. So in the mornings I would go to a massive market nearby and pick up cheap cuts of lamb and beef. I would even buy a whole pig, take it back and butcher it myself, using every bit of it to feed the men, making stews, steaks and sausages. The men seemed to love it and when I eventually left they were devastated. So I hope I managed to raise my game and produce the best food my little part of the Italian army has ever had. If you march on your stomach, then I would at least try and fill it well. What's more, I enjoyed it.

As I was on National Service and no longer in prison, I did get the usual time off at weekends. But stuck up in Como or Verona with a bunch of eighteen-year-olds I had no one to spend it with. I'd already done a lot of travelling by then, but I didn't know a single soul from northern Italy. Or did I?

One day, lying in my bunk and trying to think what I would do on my next break, I remembered a pair of warm, dark eyes from the bar at the hotel in Alba Adriatica. I remembered the wife who would sway her hips as she walked past me on the way to her room whenever her husband went out to the beach. She was from Milan, less than a hundred kilometres from my base. And I knew her address.

Everything was stacked against me meeting my Mrs Robinson again. Years had passed. She might have moved. She might have forgotten me. Her husband might open the door. I could get arrested for stalking. But it turned out that I was right to head over to Milan on my weekend off. My former lady friend opened the door and recognised me straight away, military crew cut or no military crew cut. She also said her marriage was finally ending. They'd been drifting apart for years, she said, neatly summing up what I'd known all along. And we were soon back where we wanted to be – in bed.

For one long stretch of time I'd spend Sunday after Sunday having sex with this lovely older lady in her Milan home. I practically ran from the barracks to get to the train station each week. We had the most incredible time. In the hotel room we'd had to make love quickly and quietly. Now we could take our time and make it obvious how much fun we were having.

More importantly, we could talk and laugh for hours afterwards. The only bad incident happened when her husband turned up unexpectedly one Sunday. If their marriage was really over, this probably shouldn't have been a problem. But, for whatever reason, it clearly was. I was pushed into the bedroom wardrobe, squashing myself down on top of piles of shoes and bags. And I had to stay there for nearly two hours until the coast was clear.

If this lady was cheating on her husband with me, then was I cheating on Jan with her? I told myself that I wasn't, because I'd only just started dating Jan when all this happened. Our relationship was so young, so I told myself it wasn't serious. I'd told Jan she should forget me while I was away. I thought she should carry on with her life rather than having some sort of year-long prison sentence of her own.

But she didn't walk away and she proved to be a true friend throughout my military interlude. She wrote to me all the time, passing on bits of news about London and the clubs and all our mutual friends. She even put in an occasional £5 note. It was a lot of money back then, though not wildly useful in an army barracks in Como. She even came to visit me in Milan when I had a full week of leave. It was pretty much the first time she had ever been abroad, so it was a big deal for her. And because neither of us had enough money for hotels, we had to go down to my family house in Abruzzo. So it was a big deal for me as well.

Marriage is important in Italy, and in most cases the younger you do it the better. Taking a girl home to your mother and then not marrying her isn't the thing to do. But I'd done that already with Eddie and too many other girls. So my very traditional mamma wasn't over the moon about the idea of hosting some English girl whom she rightly thought might stop me ever returning full-time to Italy.

I was in my smartest army uniform when I met Jan in Milan. When we got back to the family in Alba Adriatica, I thought I looked pretty good. But neither Jan nor anyone else seemed to agree, so there was a bit of tension about that from the start. And, while the week's holiday wasn't very relaxed, it somehow felt as if Jan and I had sealed some kind of deal by spending so much time with my family. We just hadn't yet put into words what that deal would be.

National Service did change me. It's a cliché to say that we all start the time as boys and end it as men, but in some ways that's how it felt. I think it was good for me to get the (not so) short, sharp shock of authority. Probably, I needed to learn that I couldn't have life all my own way and that I couldn't charm my way out of every bad situation. I learned that not every bill you have to pay is about money. And that sometimes you need to give up being a wilful individual for some kind of greater good.

The final lesson, for a cocky twenty-two-year-old, was that life was precious and passed quickly. I didn't want to waste another year doing something I hadn't chosen. When I came out of the barracks for the last time, I swore I'd live out my dreams, however hard they might be to achieve. And that meant getting back to London fast.

I think I broke my old mamma's heart by rejecting Italy when I regained my freedom. I didn't have the words to tell her that I would always love our country, but that I needed more than a fishing village in Abruzzo to inspire me for the rest of my life. My old boss at La Spezia turned out to be a real hero that year. He hadn't quite kept my job open for me while I was away, but he conjured up a new one for me the moment I got back to London.

The money, though, was as lousy as ever, so I was straight back into another £8-a-week room in Clapham, putting more coins in the electricity meter and peeing in the dark. This was something I knew I had to change. Once more, Jan provided the solution. She lived with her family in Stanmore in North London and they had a spare room.

If I'd thought about it for longer I would probably have stayed put: it was too early in our relationship and being with her family would complicate things. Also, I probably needed some time alone after my stint in the army. But I said yes and put my suitcase under the single bed of my new room. Jan seemed to want this and she had waited for me for a whole year, after all. I felt as if I owed it to her to play ball. But, while the two of us were still able to laugh and have fun, there were some real clouds building up over the rest of our lives.

The first problem was that Jan's house wasn't a very happy home. Her dad had left her mum just before I moved in and the atmosphere was still pretty awful. Then I got the news that my own dad had died. He'd had a stroke the previous year and had gone downhill fast, the way fit and strong men often do. Physically, he had been like a shell of a man the last time I had seen him, like a sack of flour that had seen its contents start trickling out on to the floor. But mentally he had the same rage. He had refused to admit he was ill. He took his frustration out on his wife, kicking her out of bed because he was so angry at himself.

He had been told to stop smoking, but that had made him even harder to live with. So the doctors let him start again. At the end of my last visit, my final look saw him outside the house, lighting up yet another cigarette. That's how I always remember him.

Back in London, I was getting more and more worried about my own mother. I've always loved writing and receiving letters. Texting, emailing and talking are all great, but to me nothing can beat a simple letter. They take time to write and to send and that makes them more valuable. They can last forever, which makes them priceless.

But, back then, I had the same old problems corresponding with my mother. I knew she still had to get my letters read out to her. I knew she would have to dictate her replies to one of our nosy neighbours or one of her many daughters-in-law. Talking to her on the phone was just as difficult. Our old house still didn't have a landline, so if I wanted to talk to Mamma I had to ring a local bar. That meant sending a letter a week or so beforehand to agree the date and the time. It seemed normal then, and more often than not it worked. But looking back, it was ridiculously complicated.

How would my mum cope on her own? That was my big worry after my father's death. Her relationship with my dad had never been any great love affair – no public affection, no kind words, no real warmth. But they had been bound together like the vines on the trees. Their roots were tied up together. It was hard to see one without the other, because they had supported each other for so many decades.

However hard my father had been to live with, he had always been there. I didn't want my mum to fall down and get lost now that he was gone. So I wrote and talked often of my next summer trip home, when I wanted to cook with her again. I told her I wanted to try to write some of her family recipes down, to record some of the creations that had been carried down for generations or born out of her own unique ingenuity. I wanted to give her something to look forward to. I knew how many laughs we would have in that big old kitchen as we cooked up a storm again, this time for fun rather than necessity. But, as it turned out, we wouldn't get the chance.

It was the middle of the morning when my brother called the restaurant where I worked. He said Mum had been to hospital for a check-up. Somehow I knew immediately that the results of any test would be bad. My mum was the kind of woman who always carried on. Farmers' wives did that. They never complained, they got on with things, they ran their houses and their families right up until their last days.

If my mother was in a hospital or a clinic, it must mean it was serious. I had always felt that when my mother died it would be from tiredness. From some 800 miles away, something told me that a clock was ticking. This was the end.

I walked out of La Spezia in silence – and I will eternally thank the boss, Mr Piero, for not needing me to give more than a few teary words of explanation. I'd never been on a plane before, or booked a flight, so I had no idea how to do it. I didn't know that most people went to travel agents. I just went straight to the airport and said I needed to get home fast. I was put on to a DC9 to Rome with Monarch Airways.

It was a holiday flight. I was surrounded by row after row of happy families, all excited about their trips out to the sun. I sat in total silence, tears in my eyes, blanking them all out, just willing the plane on to Italy as fast as it could fly. When I got to Rome, I had to wait five hours for a train to the coast. But my mother had waited for me. She was so small, so frail and so pale in her hospital bed. But she was proud as well. I held her hand and that was enough. We didn't need to speak. Then, soon afterwards and in peace, she drifted away and died.

That night, I was back in the thin tiny bed in the old shared room where I had spent my childhood. The same wind blew in from the Adriatic, the same waves were crashing softly on the beach. But everything had changed. I fell apart somehow, even though I was well into my twenties. Somehow, I suppose I had thought my parents were invincible. Now they had both gone within a year. And I didn't know what the hell I was doing with my life.

Perhaps for the first time, I decided to do nothing. I retreated into myself as I cried. I couldn't bring myself to engage with the world or the people around me. I didn't feel strong enough to leave that single bed by the sea in Alba Adriatica. The cooking I had wanted to do with my mother. The recipes I had wanted to write down and record for my own children one day. The ingredients I had wanted to savour and play with. I let it all fade away for three long months.

In that time, I found a photograph that I have never lost. It's black and white, and I'm holding my mother's hand and she has two of my younger nephews in her arms. Today, we all look like peasants, gypsies even. But, back then, I was my mother's little prince. It is a snapshot from another age. I can sense the pride in my mother's eyes. I can see all the strength in her face. I know her spirit will never leave me. In the good times, I hope she watches over me.

Three months is too long for a grown man to grieve. I know that now, and as the seasons changed on the Adriatic I snapped out of my gloom. I think it was the sea air that did it. It was getting colder, but there was still a big, bright Italian sky above me. It reminded me that I wanted to be alive. And, as I walked along the seafront in Alba Adriatica, I knew I felt most alive when I was in London.

I headed back by train, leaving from the same station I had used all those years earlier, when I wore my brother's cast-off trousers. As usual, plenty of my family were there to see me go. But I don't think many of them could understand what it was that called me so far away – especially to a country they hadn't seen, but which they thought was always grey, wet and cold. As my train clanked out of sunny coastal Italy, I knew they had a point. It was paradise in Abruzzo. Everyone had space to live and room to grow. Why would anyone swap that for crowded, grimy old London? Why would I?

I was smiling to myself even as I asked the question. It seemed that even thinking about London made me smile. So going back had to be the right thing to do. I started work again the moment I arrived and I found a new church to attend in Clerkenwell, where most of the congregation seemed to be Italian. Back then, it felt right to attend more often and church saw me through some bad and lonely days. In the end, it helped me find myself.

CHAPTER SEVEN

Soho

I fell in love with Soho the first time I saw it – or, should I say, the first time I smelled it. The streets were crowded, noisy and incredibly smelly. There was a warren of side streets and alleyways that housed strange-looking characters of both sexes. Street markets took up every inch of space on the bigger roads and rotting fruit was constantly being lobbed into the gutters, where it remained for days.

The modern sex trade hadn't yet started to dominate the area, though there were plenty of very dodgy doorways where you could be enticed in for a good time. What I liked most about Soho was the way all its various traders seemed to live. They knew each other. The barrow boys and the barmen all yelled obscenities at each other as they passed in the street. But you knew that when a fight broke out they'd lose their own teeth to defend each other.

In the middle of a big anonymous city, this struck me as being like a perfect Italian village. I wanted to be part of it.

I wanted those traders to know my name, to shout swear words out at me as I walked past and to fight for me if an outsider ever cut up rough. I wanted to be part of that Soho family. That was where I wanted to run my own restaurant. It was where I wanted to build my empire.

Maybe I was being cocky again (no – *of course* I was being cocky again) but the more I walked around the area, the more I felt I could do it. I saw what the other restaurants were serving and I knew I could do better. Most of the head chefs were Italian ex-coalminers, for God's sake. The other Italian restaurants all seemed to be run by Portuguese or Spanish chefs. What was worse was that the Brits didn't know the difference. These men were putting chicken kiev on the menu, charging a fortune for it and persuading Londoners that it was what we all ate in Italy.

The owners packed the punters in like sardines. You sat inches from the tables to your left and right, with other chairs pushing in on you from behind. It was simple profiteering. But the owners called it 'intimate' and 'traditional' and got away with it. Brits would queue up to pay to eat in these terrible surroundings. And, despite all the sprawling fruit-and-vegetable markets in the Soho streets, there never seemed to be a single item of fresh food on any menu. I knew I could run a better restaurant and serve better food with my eyes closed. I could hardly do worse.

The more I dreamed and planned, the more I felt the time could be right for someone like me to turn things upside down. Anyone who eats out in Britain today won't be able to imagine how awful the situation was back then – the choices and the quality were so bad. But the revolution in music and fashion that had turned the 1960s and 1970s on their head was finally on the point of hitting the restaurant scene.

A handful of new names were springing up and some of the recent arrivals were doing well. I knew I could follow suit. But how could a boy in his twenties with no experience get a restaurant of his own? I would talk about this endlessly with anyone who would listen.

'I could do better than every single one of those other restaurants,' I'd say.

But how? As it turned out, something else would get in the way before I had the chance. Jan and I were going to get married. We were back in Italy the year after my mum had died and the rest of my family seemed to have multiplied like bloody rabbits. If I couldn't seem to count all my various brothers and sisters-in-law and the like, then I've no idea how Jan coped. And in the coupled-up, two-by-two atmosphere of Italy, it suddenly became clear that we were supposed to tie the knot as well.

The local consensus was that I was far too old to be single. So my brothers and their wives decided everything and Jan and I were just swept along on the tide. The one thing that a corner of my mind clung to was the fact that it couldn't, surely, be possible to arrange a wedding so suddenly. We were only on holiday, after all. Surely, if we really planned to get married we would have to get a lot of paperwork done? For once, I was grateful for the mad Italian bureaucracy. But I had forgotten one simple fact: my brother was a priest. So anything was possible and things did move very fast.

Jan and I married in Alba Adriatica and it cost a fortune, even in cheap, coastal Italy. Jan and I didn't even have enough cash to buy two plane tickets back to London. So she and her mother flew back and I came home on my old motorbike.

I left a day before they did, but despite several huge rain storms along the way I got back to Jan's doorstep in London at exactly the same time as her.

I hated being broke. 'One day,' I swore, 'one day I'm going to arrive in this country with a decent amount of cash in my pocket.' Not that I was doing too badly, truth be told. Before the wedding Piero, my boss at La Spezia, had helped me get a mortgage for a £13,000 flat in Sudbury, near Wembley. So Jan and I had somewhere to start our married life together. But, as usual, there was a problem. Jan's mother didn't want to live on her own. She had sold up in North London and moved in with us.

Every morning the second woman I saw was my mother-in-law, fast asleep on the living-room sofa. Every morning I would quietly shake my head, confused. Why wasn't I paying attention when this happened? I'd been sleepwalking and had somehow got married in a daze. Now this. Why were so many things in my life being taken out of my own control?

Out of nowhere, I decided that running a restaurant would be the best way to get that control back. It would give me my own world. I was ready for it.

CHAPTER EIGHT

My First Restaurant

Before leaving for Italy, I had landed a job at Il Siciliano on Dean Street in Soho. It was a classic of its kind, the most traditional of places – frescoed landscapes on the walls; thick tablecloths on the tables; dark alcoves where you could sit undisturbed for hours; and long, thick menus that sometimes even resembled genuine Italian cooking. Il Siciliano was owned by an inspirational man called Walter – another older mentor who would change my life.

Walter gave me room to breathe and find my own place in his restaurant. He let me carve out an ideal role, leading in the kitchen but spending as much extra time as possible front-of-house. That way I could talk to the customers, see what they liked and what they didn't. When plates left the tables empty, I asked why. If they came back half-eaten or less, I asked why as well. Customers didn't seem to mind. In fact, I think they seemed to like a bit of contact with their host. They liked being treated with a bit of respect. The customer was still a long way from being king in London. Eating out was still just a minority sport and, however much money people were spending (and however bad the food they were being served), they seemed to expect to be treated like naughty children: seen but not heard.

In Il Siciliano, I was the naughty child instead. It paid off. As my confidence rose, I would laugh and joke with some of the regulars. Other newcomers saw how much fun we were having and I think they wanted to join the in-crowd as well. So they came back a few times, became regulars themselves and got to join in on the next set of jokes. Repeat that several times and most days you end up with a room full of laughter.

If you are flexible enough in the kitchen, you also get a menu that people actually enjoy. Running a successful restaurant really doesn't have to be rocket science. Just fall in love with the people you're cooking for and do everything you can to make them have a great time.

Just before my unexpectedly extended wedding trip to Italy, Il Siciliano had been booming like never before and while I don't want to boast I think the room probably fell a bit flat when I was away. But, by the time I got back to London, Walter had got used to coping on his own and I found a new opening at a different restaurant, Du Rollo, just around the corner on Greek Street. It was three times the size, modern and french but with an italian chef that I was to learn a lot from. And it had another wonderful owner. Peter du Rollo was a local legend, a huge Soho character. He lived a big life and showed me that restaurants could be rock and roll. I liked it.

As I tried to impress Peter, I got lucky. Someone from the old Il Siciliano days had spotted me walking into the restaurant on Greek Street. He came in to ask where I had been and why I had moved and booked in for lunch the next day. We had a great time catching up as I did my usual darts from kitchen to front-of-house. Then, another set of my old customers made the switch to my new place. And another. I was twenty-six years old and I seemed to have a following.

Against all the odds, Du Rollo was bursting at the seams – and Il Siciliano was probably looking pretty empty. So I wasn't looking forward to the conversation when Walter came round to see me in the lull of one afternoon.

'Ciao, Aldo. Busy day?'

'Yes, it's been pretty good.'

'I'm told you're doing well in the evenings as well?'

'We're lucky, yes. We're pretty full.'

'We're dead on Dean Street.'

For once in my life I was lost for words. I didn't know what he expected me to say. Fortunately, he spoke first.

'I'm too old for this game. I just want to go off and play some golf and forget all about it.'

There was another long pause as I looked out of the windows on to Greek Street and tried to guess where this conversation might be going.

Then Walter came right out and said it. 'Do you want to rent my restaurant? It's yours for £500 a week.'

I said yes without pausing for breath. We shook hands on the deal then and there. I'd not done a single sum in my head to work out if I could afford it or if it would add up. All I could see was the thought of having my own proper place. I wouldn't just be the chef or the good guy out front-of-house who always had to defer to the owner or the manager. For £500 a week, at Il Siciliano, I would be the boss and I'd make the rules. I was twenty-six and I was fearless. I was probably a bit stupid as well. Bearing all that in mind, how could I possibly say no?

Walter wanted out fast, so I had no time to worry about what I had taken on. Jan and I tracked down some friends, Nino came back from Spain to help and we all had a painting party the first weekend. The idea was to try to spruce up some of the interiors for the minimum amount of money. That way, it would at least feel as if there had been a new start the following week. But we had to keep everything else the same: the tables, chairs, china, cutlery and kitchen equipment. My main task was to focus on the menu and the atmosphere.

When it came to food, all I wanted to do was simple, great Italian food in season. But would British people understand what it was? That's when I learned the power of two distinct groups of people – celebrities and the local people working in the media. They tended to have travelled far more than your average Brit back then. They were more open to new things. Ultimately, they could make Italian food cool. They could make sure ordinary people bought it. Celebrities were worth courting, I decided. And at last I had a restaurant of my own to woo them into.

Well, I would as long as I had enough staff. Everyone at Il Siciliano had been happy enough when I had been an employee there, bringing plenty of high-tipping customers into the dining room. But not even the thought of more big tips could make them happy with the idea of this youngster being their boss. So they left – almost all of them. I put the word out and tried to fill all the gaps as I woke up to the other responsibilities of my new role. I wouldn't just be cooking and serving the food. I'd have to buy it as well.

My Triumph TR6 days were long gone, but I squeezed together every penny I could find to buy a blue Fiat 500 instead. That way I could do the early-morning market runs myself. In the process, I entered one of London's amazing secret worlds. The old Billingsgate was still the place for fish, Covent Garden had the fruit and veg and Smithfield the meat.

Apart from anything else, they were amazing structures, beautiful old buildings with a hundred corners and corridors you could get lost in. I'm so pleased none has been demolished and replaced by glass office blocks. But what made them unique were the people inside them – the porters, the traders, the old-timers and the characters. It couldn't have been more intimidating to me, the boy from Italy who was less than half as old as most of them.

But at least I'd worked the fish shop in Alba Adriatica as a kid. I knew what I was buying and I wouldn't be ripped off. I'd also take a deep breath and try to join in some of their banter – putting on my awful cockney accent sometimes to try to win some laughs. In the process, thankfully, I won some respect as well.

The markets were all cash-only businesses back then and everything was bartered for. But the fact that my menu at Il Siciliano would change every day helped me here. I had no set demands every morning when I arrived at Billingsgate, then Covent Garden then Smithfield. I would buy what I liked or what I could afford. Then, when I got back to Dean Street, I would do what my mother had taught me. I would be creative, I'd use my ingenuity; I would make the best of what I had.

At dawn one day at the fish market, the guys gave me a load of shark for free because they couldn't sell it to anyone else. I loaded it into my little Fiat and I couldn't have been happier. I put it on my menu. I did the patter front-of-house and I sold shark meat for £7 or £8 a portion. Marinated in a little olive oil, lemon and fresh basil, then barbecued, they were tender and tasted wonderful. No one put squid on a menu back then but I did. And I sold out of that as well. I'd buy sardines and mackerel for £2 or £3 a case and sell it for £5 a plate, stuffed with fresh herbs and roasted. Simple, fresh and delicious. No other restaurant in London was selling sardines back then, but I knew it would bring me huge profits and that customers would like it if they could only be persuaded to try it. I was the one to persuade them. I was chef, maitre d' and chief salesman. And I was loving it all.

Some of the other challenges of working in Soho were less good, though. The old Maltese mafia were at the tail end of their reign and I had to deal with them for the first time, with no idea of what any other local business did. It was a subject no one talked about but everyone had to face up to. Maybe as an Italian I should have been used to protection rackets, but I wasn't. It was tough because I was no longer protected by Walter, an ex-boxer. So I just handed over the minimum amount of cash I could get away with. I offered these mysterious guys free meals and hoped it would all go away. Fortunately, over the years, it did.

Far better neighbours were moving in all over Soho, which may well be why the old Mafioso types were ultimately squeezed out. Sony were in Soho Square and the film, advertising and music industries was swooping on the big, empty office spaces in what had been a seedy and forgotten part of town. They reckoned it had colour and I couldn't have agreed more.

It was the start of real expense-account lunches and these sharply dressed men and women had cash to spare. Unfortunately, the law made it hard to relieve them of as much of it as I wanted. You couldn't serve alcohol in the afternoons back then. So we served wine and spirits in coffee cups to try to hide it. Anything to keep the customers spending.

'I'm pregnant.' Jan told me the news in the £13,000 Sudbury flat that was taking up all the rest of our money and giving us sleepless nights. A property, £500 a week for a restaurant, protection money to the mafia and now a baby. Could we survive all this? I was genuinely excited to be a father, though I probably didn't know exactly what it would really mean. But I had so much else to worry about. Those days are a blur. I blocked a lot out so I could keep all the plates spinning.

Less than six months into my time at Il Siciliano and business was suddenly fantastic. We had reached some kind of critical mass. I'd poached Franco, the old chef from Du Rollo, and we could serve up to fifty covers in a sitting. We were still working with a skeleton crew, just me and Franco in the kitchen, two others front-of-house. But we had got rid of the old sweet trolley and the Black Forest gateau and introduced so many more modern – and more profitable – alternatives: zabaglione, cooked in front of the customer, tiramisu, panna cotta... And the money was rolling in.

After another six months, I ditched my old Fiat – not least because it stank of raw fish, so I pity the poor sod who bought it from me. Amazingly, I worked out that I could afford a Porsche. And because I suddenly felt that image was all and that success might breed success, I decided to get one. It was the second non-Italian car I had ever owned, and I felt bad about that. But I wanted to be flash. It was the 1980s, greed was soon going to be good and I was going to be a winner.

As the years passed, Walter became well aware of how buzzing his old restaurant had become. But I didn't have to feel sorry for him as he worked on his golf swing and worried about what might have been. He still owned the restaurant's freehold and because of the success we had created it had soared in value as well. Everyone was winning back then. Surely it would never end?

CHAPTER NINE

Wine Bars and Wild Nights

From the start of the Dean Street adventure, I had been renting a flat above the restaurant. Without it, I would never have made it in from Sudbury to do the market runs at dawn every day. But I kept it on even after I splashed out on a new manager and passed a lot of the early-morning responsibilities on to him. Looking back, it was a flash and extravagant thing to do. But I was feeling flash and extravagant. I had a top business and I was succeeding.

Every other restaurant owner in Soho seemed ancient to me. I was still in my mid-twenties and I was running rings around them, riding the new wave of having a buzzing, theatrical dining room rather than some silent old relic from the 1950s. The way I saw it, I was in central London, I had a set of restaurant keys in my pocket and I was living the *vida loca*. It could have gone on like that forever, but I started to party a bit too hard and I took my eye off the ball. Less than three years after hitting gold with Il Siciliano, I started to make mistakes.

The first one was the biggest. I bought a wine bar.

Strange, really, for someone who had hardly ever drunk alcohol in his life! There's this myth about big, happy Italian families who teach their children to drink wine from a young age and avoid the binge-drinking culture we're so obsessed with in Britain. But big, happy Italian families who drank at dinner tended to have at least a little bit of money to spare. My family didn't. We made wine on the farm, but we sold it. I remember my dad drinking a little bit just before Christmas. I remember me getting a taste from his glass only once. But that was it. In London I didn't drink either. At first, I couldn't afford to. Then I realised I was pretty much high on the life I was leading. I didn't need booze to take me any further. That would come a lot later.

So why buy a wine bar?

For the same reason I went to Germany, to the South of France and even to the beach as a boy: to chase pretty women. I was married and my lovely daughter Laura had been born the previous year. But I was still the kid in the candy store. It was wrong, but I couldn't spend too many evenings up in Sudbury when there was so much to see down in the West End. So, when one of my customers told me about a place called Maynards on Woodstock Street in Mayfair, I couldn't resist.

Wine bars were it, back then. They were the absolute place to go – or, more importantly, for women to go. When I headed south of Oxford Street to take a look at Maynards and saw the kind of women who went there, I knew instantly that it was for me. The bar was a couple of doors down from Christie's the auctioneers. It was the key party place for all those tall, posh English gals from the Home Counties. Daddy had bought them all flats in West London and nippy little cars to get around London in.

It was probably a case of opposites attract, but these were just the kind of girls this short, cocky young Italian lad wanted to meet. I must have been mad, but I used the cash I was making at Il Siciliano to buy Maynards outright. All I had ever wanted was to own a restaurant. Instead, I was renting a restaurant and had bought a wine bar. I should have known things would go wrong. I should have realised how young and foolish I still was.

Maynards had a big ground-floor area with a small basement room below. It was lively, but I knew I could move it up a gear. I threw in some of the party atmosphere that had worked so well over on Dean Street. But this time there was a dangerous difference. In Maynards, I was part of the party. This was my hobby and it would prove to be ridiculously expensive.

I loved being the man in charge at lunchtime when the office girls tottered in, all high heels, high voices and clouds of expensive perfume. Their male admirers crowded around as well and at lunchtimes everyone paid their bills. The businessman in me ensured we had good mark-ups on the wine, made a bit of extra on some food and had plenty of money to count in the afternoons. In the early evenings, the after-work crowd were just as flash with their cash and I was a happy and temporarily rich man. But then I'd take my eye off the ball. I'd head out with some of the guests to someone else's club for a change of scene in the middle of the evening. I would spend far too much money there – never getting anything for nothing, interestingly enough. Then I'd invite anyone and everyone back to Maynards, where I'd always put the first set of bottles on the house. By the time everyone was in a real party mood, it was normally closing-up time.

Licensing laws were still tough and you couldn't sell booze after 11pm. Not a problem, I decided. I was having such a good time that, if I couldn't sell booze, I would just give it away. Anything to keep the good times rolling. We started having wild lock-ins. Everyone partied until 6am in the basement bar, where the police couldn't see us. By the time the last of the guests left the following morning, the wine fridge was as empty as the cash drawer.

But I couldn't have cared less. No wonder Maynards became such a hot place to party – I was the most generous host in town. Basically, all the money we made every day had to be spent refilling our stocks the following morning – all the money and more. But still the party went on. I was having too much fun to count the costs. I liked being able to get so many of London's cool people around me. I didn't let myself face up to the fact that by opening up my wine fridges I was really paying for everyone's company. I wouldn't acknowledge this for many years.

Fortunately, there were a few times back then when I remembered I was a married man with a child and I did try to get more serious. I revamped the bar-food menu one time to try to bring in some more cash at lunchtime and in the early evenings. But wine bars were really just about the booze, so I soon let it slip again.

For months and months, Il Siciliano was doing so well that it didn't seem to matter that so much cash was pouring out of Maynards. I upgraded my car again to try to compete with some of the posh boys in Mayfair. I made a rule that I would only have beautiful female staff. And I seriously let things slip on Dean Street. I had long since stopped doing the morning market run; my new late-night lifestyle made it out of the question. But, because I was no longer in control of the food coming into the restaurant, I had less to do with what went out.

I didn't get the buzz out of creating great new dishes out of some of the strange purchases. I was getting a wine-induced buzz elsewhere and that felt like enough. Worse, I was incredibly unprofessional in front of the staff and customers when I was in Il Siciliano. My flat was still above the shop, so I would stumble past everyone, often still drunk, normally hung-over, always dishevelled and reeking of booze and smoke. All my staff were fantastic. They could have taken advantage of me – perhaps they should have. But they carried on, doing their jobs even though they didn't exactly get much in the way of strong leadership.

And still my partying continued. In fact, it moved up a gear. I was about to meet George Michael.

George's old friend and former band-mate David Austin had become a close friend of mine after spending so much time in Il Siciliano and Maynards. He brought George and Andrew Ridgeley over just as Wham!-mania was at its height.

'George likes caviar,' David told me – maybe seriously, maybe joking – just before that first dinner.

Not wanting to risk a mistake, I went out and spent more than £500 on caviar just in case. And that first time, George buggered off at the end of the night assuming that someone else had paid the bill. Everyone else thought George had paid up, so my staff were left with a big hole in the accounts. Still, at least we'd had a great night. And it was going to be the first of very many more.

What I loved about George and Andrew wasn't just their songs (I knew every word) or their own good company. It was the beautiful women they both brought with them. Early on, I had no idea that George was gay – though, in my defence, he reckons he wasn't so sure himself back then. Anyway, he certainly had his share of stunning women.

He and Andrew seemed to be competing on that front from the start. After the caviar incident, our next big night was at a birthday party for George's cousin Andros, someone else who would become a close friend. Then came all the other lunches, dinners and parties – including all the times when the post-Wham! George took control of our karaoke machine and happily belted out 'I Want Your Sex' between every couple of tracks. He's a brilliant DJ and always wanted to take charge of the music at our parties.

In the quieter times, the more I talked to George the more I realised how on the edge he was. He was a mixed-up man who both loved and hated being the centre of attention. I also noticed that he was always being watched. It wasn't just the paparazzi, the press and the fans. It was all his music colleagues and the industry workers, and his family and friends as well.

The Italian village boy in me recognised something in the Greek Cypriot crew that always seemed to surround George. He spent a lot of time with Andros and loads of their other relatives were always around as well. When he was with those people, I thought George should have been at his most relaxed, but even then there was tension. They were keeping an eye on him and he seemed to know it. I'd experienced the pressure that comes from big southern European families and I was certain that George felt it too.

George's home, up in Hampstead, was like a giant glass house. We would all end up there for parties and to chill out after yet another big night on the town. Yes, it was shielded from the street by big, thick walls. But a glass house certainly didn't suit a man who seemed to be constantly hiding.

Meanwhile, I had a new flat above the restaurant in Dean Street, where I stayed for far too many nights. Laura was now growing up in the super-safe suburb of Pinner – a mad two-hour drive from the restaurant on the days I picked her up from school. Back in London, David Austin became a temporary lodger when he was having problems with a house move, so George became an even more frequent visitor and a bigger part of my life.

By then, I'd also spotted something else that would soon become common knowledge. That Andrew Ridgeley, far from being Wham!'s silent partner, was actually the cool part of the group. He was the one who really got the girls. George – whom we all called Yog – was starting to spend all his time with this one stunningly beautiful Japanese girl. But he always had barriers up. It would take me a little while longer to find out why.

CHAPTER TEN

Meeting Freddie

Another of my regulars at Il Siciliano was the singer Peter Straker. He was one of Freddie Mercury's many ex-boyfriends and always had some wild and wonderful people at his tables. One night, he booked the whole restaurant out for a big private party. I loved those nights. Guaranteed good times. Guaranteed money in the till. And this was going to be a cracker.

Freddie was one of the first to arrive. He was really soberly dressed, as he almost always was off-stage. That night he had a plain white shirt and ordinary black trousers. He could have been a bank manager. Except perhaps for the moustache. As expected, it was a fantastic night. The actress Stephanie Beacham was another great guest. I was lusting after her in *Dynasty* and she was just as glamorous and regal in real life. And she's got a really dirty laugh, which I love.

The other big thing about the party was that at one point Freddie tried to burn the restaurant down. Maybe that's why we got to be such good friends. If you can get over something like that on the night you first meet, you can pretty much get over anything!

It happened at 4am. The big bowls of pasta I had made had long since disappeared and Freddie was hungry again, so he headed off to forage for food in my kitchens. He decided he wanted some chips and that he could cook them himself while everyone else carried on partying. Unfortunately, he forgot to put oil in the chip pan and then forgot about it altogether. A rush of flame set off the fire alarms and nearly destroyed the restaurant. For Freddie – or Melina, as he liked to be called – the incident was twice as embarrassing because he never knowingly ended a party.

He was reserved with everyone at first; I guess he had to be. But, if he liked you, then he liked you. And he liked to have fun. We hit all the clubs together back then and I was like a rabbit in the headlights, dazzled by this wildly camp figure who rushed on ahead, kissed just about everybody and never stopped looking for a better party somewhere else. But for all that high-voltage excitement there was another side to Freddie. Sometimes he would be with the quieter group in a corner, talking about anything and everything.

Freddie was always trying to stay ahead of trends and spot what could make a great new sound. He always listened to the music when we were out at clubs and he asked everyone's opinions. He was catty, bitchy and hilarious. But he was also a very real, very thoughtful man. Sometimes, I think every famous person I have ever met is several different personalities all wrapped up in one.

Freddie certainly was – and I really enjoyed seeing his quieter side. I was at his house in Kensington once when he had just got back from a working visit to Spain. For such a glamorous man, Freddie didn't have a particularly glitzy home. Kensington wasn't a palace, just a place to party.

That night he was even more animated than usual, buzzing with excitement about a new track he was working on. He wouldn't leave the piano all night. It was there that I heard 'Barcelona' the first time, sung and played by Freddie in his own living room. It was breathtaking for all of us – him included – which showed just how much he believed in the song.

Freddie's house in Kensington was party central. Some nights, for security reasons, his doors and gates were locked once we were all inside so it was, quite literally, impossible to leave. I'm not ashamed to say I loved every minute of it. I was a restaurant owner. I was cool. I was so very in with the most in-crowd in town and I'm not going to pretend I didn't milk it for all it was worth.

But there was a problem. I wasn't just another one of Freddie Mercury's friends. I was also a restaurant owner, a dad and a husband. When one party was over, Freddie and his gang could probably sleep right through till the next one. But I was supposed to scrub floors, check inventories, mark up menus, pep up my staff and run through the books. Sometimes I'd leave Freddie's house at 6am and try to clear my head as I paced back to Dean Street with another long day and night of work ahead.

Some nights we all needed to detox from the partying and we hit upon a great routine to do it. When we went out in a small group, we would often head to Browns on

Great Queen Street to dance. From Browns, a group of us would often go on to Champney's health club on Piccadilly. We'd all sit in the steam room beside the underground swimming pool. We would sweat out the night's excesses until the morning rush hour had passed. 'I don't know why we're paying for our houses. We could live like this every day,' I told the gang after one long steam. And, for a while, it seemed as if we were.

Freddie, meanwhile, carried on flitting in and out of Il Siciliano and all our other favourite haunts. I think his image scared a lot of people off, so he didn't get approached as often as he might have been in the street or in a club. People thought that if they asked him for an autograph he might get bitchy and let the insults fly. But it wouldn't have been his style.

He was relaxed enough to go most places with just a driver acting as a sort of minder. And, however outrageous he was with us, he was never rude to his fans. At least not to their faces – he often gave a bit of commentary on what they were wearing or what he might like to do to them in bed as they walked away.

Freddie was also surrounded much of the time by the other band members from Queen. It was obvious that they were all close friends – and, as Freddie got thinner and frailer, this would be more important than ever. My favourite of the group was Brian May, a man who acted like a mad professor sometimes. He was like a musical genius who seemed to think everyone shared his interests and obsessions. His equally shaggy partner Anita Dobson was great too. She is a lot posher than that rough old bird she played in *EastEnders*.

One final thing set Freddie apart from too many of the other celebrities I have met. He paid his bills – and more. When he hosted a party in Il Siciliano's private room, he picked up the tab. When he and some mates had a meal, he never left without paying for it and the staff loved him because he always tipped high. It was as if his feet had never fully left the ground. He remembered that ordinary people had livings to earn and books to balance.

Unfortunately for me, that wasn't how a lot of other people saw it. The more famous some people are, and the more money they have, the meaner they seem to be. Some seem so unused to paying for anything that they've forgotten why or how they should ever do so. Maybe they think their managers will sort it all out afterwards. Maybe they think that, by turning up to some bar, restaurant or club, they are giving it so much publicity that they don't have to pay. But publicity won't pay our wine suppliers, our fish bills or our electricity costs. If we need to fill forty covers to break even, we can't give eight of them away for free.

Who else was in the party crowd back then? Who wasn't? I was good friends with pop writer Paul Simper, so he brought a whole load of other stars to the restaurant. We partied with Kylie Minogue, the Bros boys and the Bananarama girls. I got to know Dave Stewart and hosted a great party for Annie Lennox at the height of her Eurythmics fame. I thought she had the sharpest, clearest voice I had ever heard. In person, she is as beautiful as a china doll, but you could tell she was uncomfortable being a star. She never played the celebrity card, never had an entourage. She is the one who proves that if you are truly talented you can keep your private life intact.

The wild crowd that made up Frankie Goes To Hollywood were the next big group to help put us on the map. Unlike George Michael, there was no mistaking their sexuality. They gawped at the best-looking of our waiters and the other diners and gave us all some mealtimes to remember. Paul Rutherford turned into a real friend, but all the others were great value as well.

I don't think I have ever had a problem accepting gay people. I like to think that Italians are so pre-programmed to be flirtatious that we'll cosy up to a lamppost if there's nothing else to work on. In the 1980s, I was so happy all the time that I had no problem flirting with Paul or any of the others. I tell people I love them all the time, men and women alike, and I mean it. I'm a happy man and I can fall in love at the drop of a hat, with an atmosphere, a mood and an occasion if not an actual person. So I've never cared who is in my restaurants or who becomes my friend, as long as they make us all feel alive and make me smile.

Out of the limelight two women became close friends – though nothing more. One was Jeanette Calliva, pretty much the leader of our party pack. She married a Sicilian guy and is today the youngest-looking mum of three big children I know. After moving on to Chinawhite years later, she also became one of the best-connected people in town.

Then there was the singer June Montana. We clicked the first day we met. Everyone thought we were having an affair because we got on so well. But we never did. It's the same with all my closest female friends. Getting up to the line but never crossing made us stronger. June and I have been through good and bad together over the past couple of decades and I wouldn't ever want to threaten that.

I suppose the businessman in me always knew the value of having pop stars and famous names in my restaurants. And, for all the jokes and the clowning around, I have always been a businessman at heart. But it wasn't just the money and the bottom line that attracted me. If you ask if I was star-struck, then I put my hand straight up and say yes. I was a kid from another country, living in a big city that I could never have imagined as a child. And I was meeting my heroes and heroines on a daily basis. So, yes, I was star-struck. I was meeting celebrities. I was so excited some days that I could barely breathe.

Forget the bank manager. I loved the fact that famous people were in my restaurant, eating my food. And I found them endlessly interesting. I'd never wanted to be locked away in a thousand-degree kitchen all day when I had customers to chat to (or chat up) in my dining room. My role as a restaurant owner was always to focus on the overall experience, to welcome people, to talk and gossip with them, to make sure they were happy and to recognise them on their next visit. My idea was that my restaurant would be like a giant family room where everyone could relax. Seeing someone like George Michael in my family room would never stop being a thrill.

But was I going to have to give it all up? Walter and I had shaken hands on the deal that I would run Il

Siciliano for six years. They had flown by in a haze of parties, easy money and good times. But then Walter came back. He must have got bored playing golf and was maybe inspired by how well his old haunt was doing. So he said he wanted it back.

Overnight, I looked set to lose the restaurant. Sure, I would be left with a wine bar that could have been squeezed for more money if I'd been interested enough. But my heart wasn't in that. I didn't want to just be a bar owner, however tall and posh my female clientele would be. I was a chef. I had to stay a restaurateur.

In life, I think some people are lucky and have a final self-protective layer that can kick in just before they would self-destruct. Others don't. Over the years I have seen too many of the latter follow drink and drugs down the wrong roads. Somehow, I've not gone that way. I seem to have had the self-protective gene, even if it's waited until the very last moment to show itself.

So, in 1988, I made the right decision about my future. I remembered the boy from the mountains who had been so happy in his mother's kitchen. I remembered that cooking had been my refuge from the farm and from my father. I remembered the respect I thought I had got at the toughest London food markets. I remembered my wife and my child. So I picked kitchens over wine bars. I wanted a restaurant business. I decided to sell Maynards before it sunk me and I got lucky by coming out of the deal with a £100,000 profit. Business prices had been soaring while I'd been out partying. My luck had been in. What I wanted now was another restaurant. Ten doors down from Il Siciliano, I found one.

CHAPTER ELEVEN

My Own Room

Othello at 41 Dean Street was one of the last old-time, old-style Italian restaurants in Soho. I could hardly know it better – I'd hung out with a lot of its staff on my first few trips to London. All that time later, it was for sale. And I had easily enough money left over to buy it.

Everything in my life got back on track after that. I felt a huge surge of enthusiasm for the place. And I had plenty to do. My job wasn't just to prove that I could run this restaurant. My role didn't stop at changing the menu and adding a new lick of paint. This time I was the owner. I could change anything and everything; I could make the place my own. This time it would be serious. All my friends shared my new enthusiasm and Nino and all my other chef pals seemed to feel that an old friend was back. I don't think they had ever really liked the wine-bar king.

I wanted a totally fresh start with Othello. I wanted to close it, refurbish it and reopen it as a whole new place. But it was a big job. It was tatty, dilapidated and showing its age. In the end, the only thing left from its old life would be the floor. It's actually a stunningly rich marble floor. Take a look today and you'll see how weathered and warm it is. I became incredibly focused on the transformation, living through an early version of all of today's home-improvement television shows as we went over budget, made mistakes and saw every simple job get horribly delayed.

One thing I got right back then – though I say so myself – was to put my own name above the door. Being Aldo Zilli had always got me a long way. It had got me noticed in England and I knew that was something I could trade upon.

'What's your name?'

'Zilli.'

'Silly?'

'No, Zilli.'

'Your name's Mr Silly?'

If I'd had a pound for every time I'd gone through that one, I could have got Othello kitted out using the best builders in town. As it was, I had to rely on the only builders I could afford – and I saw them drinking in Dean Street pubs far more often than I saw them at work in my new business. So what exactly would I call the old Othello if I ever got it open? I thought of so many different combinations of my name, but in the end I decided to keep it simple. Signor Zilli seemed hugely arrogant. It sounded a bit like an old man's restaurant, a place owned by someone with a reputation as long as a lifetime. I was a baby in restaurant terms back in 1988.

But what the hell.

I wanted my name above the door and, while I agreed that Mr Zilli's might get mocked, I felt that Signor Zilli would get remembered.

I also had one other weapon in my armoury – my lifelong love of talking to customers and finding out more about what they do. I was helped out here after taking to so many of the new breed of advertising staff who had always treated Il Siciliano like their office canteen.

You could always spot the advertising people. Their clothes, their haircuts and even their glasses were so different. Over the years, I had listened in on loads of conversations about the pitches they had won and lost, the campaigns they had launched and the work they had done. In the afternoons, serving them illicit wine in coffee cups, I'd often sat down and heard more. Advertising people were always ready to talk, so I reckon I had a bit of a headstart on some other restaurant owners. I knew a bit about creating an image or a brand.

I doodled on bits of paper. I looked up at what seemed like a million other shop and restaurant fronts to see what worked and what didn't. Then I finally got it. I created a sort of logo, writing the word Zilli with the two 'll's running through the word and the two 'i's upside down. There was something upside down about having a name like Zilli in the first place, so I thought it worked. Somehow, the whole thing reminded me of the sea and of happy times. Since then, I have never once wanted to change that design. If I was doing it all again today, those scrawls on a napkin would probably have cost me hundreds of thousands of pounds in fees to some marketing company. But back in 1988, while I had the name and the logo, would I ever have the actual restaurant to go with it?

On the rare occasions when I could get my builders out of the pub, they kept finding more and more work that needed to be done. In the end, I told them to focus on the ground-floor room; we could do a soft opening and expand into the basement later. We didn't have any spare cash for much of a party on opening night. But all I wanted were happy, noisy people who could act as living advertisements of my arrival. I got them and for the first few weeks we had plenty of bums on seats.

Problem was, that we had just one useable toilet. Night after night with a maximum of just twenty diners in the room, it seemed as if they always wanted to use the loo at exactly the same bloody time.

'What is it with English bladders?' I'd scream at my kitchen staff, mortified at the queues. 'Didn't their mothers tell them to go before they left home?'

All chefs want to sell a lot of drink, because so much of your profits can come from it. But part of me wanted to keep the restaurant hot and dry back then. Anything to stop people needing to pee! Even serving watery soup seemed a big risk until we had at least one more toilet in working order.

More seriously, I worried that I might have miscalculated the launch. I still wanted to be known as a generous host. I was serving complimentary nibbles like bruschetta, dips and spiced sardines with the menus. But the economics of restaurants are harsh. Everything costs you money, starting long before your first member of staff arrives for their shift. I needed the covers from the basement room to help pay for all the costs of running the twenty seats upstairs. But it was costing more and more to get that basement room ready and I would be in the red until it did.

It was a vicious circle and for the first time in my life I couldn't talk my way out of it. I had spent every penny of my wine-bar money and I needed another £30,000 to get Signor Zilli finished. But it could as well have been £3 million. I had no experience of borrowing from banks, because until now I'd always lived on my easy cash flow.

I did get one useful windfall back then. One of my regulars in the restaurant was a shaggy-haired advertising man called Trevor Beatty. He asked me to front a commercial for chewing gum. Ultimately, it would be the first of many commercials for me. But back then I was terrified. We filmed it in a mocked-up kitchen in a studio and I was so nervous it took me about 100 takes to get right. Still the money tided me over for a while, though that soon ran out as well.

Being in debt meant that, for the first time since those very early days in London, I felt like an outsider. But, back then, I'd got a buzz out of the feeling – I'd seen it as a challenge to break into this big, noisy new city. Now all I could see were walls blocking me in. All I could think of was that I was going to fail. Signor Zilli would have to close before it had properly opened.

And how all the old-timers would laugh. This upstart, cocky youngster from a cheap and cheerful tourist town would be getting his just deserts, they would say. The best he could hope for now was another rented restaurant with a proper chef's name above the door.

My friend David Austin came through for me back then, when he realised just how desperate I was. It was in the half-finished Signor Zilli where we talked, deep into one afternoon after he had watched the long loo queues at lunch. I showed him the wonky walls and the building site that was under our feet. I told him about my dreams for the place and how good I knew it could be.

'How much do you need to get it finished?'

Nine words. But they were my lifeline. In life, I think you meet very few good friends, very few true friends. David is one of mine. He understood me and he shared my dream. So he gave me the money I needed, even though he was desperately hard up himself and didn't really have any cash to spare. It was a lot more than the handful of lire my mother had given me from my father's hiding place all those years ago on Alba Adriatica station. But it bought me exactly the same freedom. And, just as in Munich, I had vowed to work wherever and whenever to earn my mother's money back, so I vowed to work to repay David. He was my first bank. I wouldn't break him.

CHAPTER TWELVE

Success

Life went mad when we had both the upstairs and downstairs rooms as Signor Zilli opened for business. From pop and cinema royalty to rock-solid real royalty, it turned out that anyone who is anyone would eat, drink and party with me there. But for me it was no longer just about having fun. I fell back in love with food. I became obsessed with fresh ingredients, just as I had when I first came to London.

Back then, I could never understand why the only fish this sea-faring nation seemed to eat was covered in batter and wrapped in yesterday's newspapers. Now I finally had the chance to try to change that. Being in the restaurant business was wonderful, all over again. And what made it all so much more fun was that I was always surrounded by people with similar dreams. Antonio Carluccio was one of them. He sold me wine from the back of his car, with his dog sitting barking on the passenger seat. Years later, after he met Priscilla and set up the Carluccio's chain, Antonio would be a huge part of London's food scene. Back then, we were just two people fighting the system and trying to get ahead.

All my other friends were just as passionate about food and restaurants. Nino was back alongside me after a spell working on the Continent and my whole team was pulling together for something we all believed could be wonderful. We were right. We still are.

Every penny we had thrown at the basement room at Signor Zilli turned out to have been well spent. It was a private place where people could get away from prying eyes and let their hair down. Some of my famous-name diners loved the paparazzi and the cameras. They wanted to be front row centre in the window upstairs, where the whole world could see how gorgeous they were. Others wanted to keep themselves – or their companions – out of sight. Signor Zilli catered for both needs.

Dealing with the paparazzi was the next big challenge I had, as 41 Dean Street became known as a star-magnet. I only ever tipped them off about a celebrity guest once. And, as it backfired on me, I soon learned how important it was to be discreet.

It was in the middle of the lunchtime service when I got a call from a newspaper journalist. He wanted to do a feature on the restaurant and I blurted out that he should come round straight away because we had the world's most famous singer sitting by the bar. I never thought he would take me seriously – or that one photographer would attract another, who would in turn attract a whole army.

When you see the sheer size of the media machine, the rows of paps who can turn up some days, you realise how scary it can be. I was starting to love having my own photo taken as a 'friend of the stars'. But I don't think I'd have liked it every day, or in such intensity. So how were George and Co. going to cope with the monster I had accidentally unleashed into the heart of Soho? All our diners were getting nervous. The photographers were lined up and practically fighting pedestrians for space on the Dean Street pavement.

My next restaurant, Zilli Fish, would have a side door that celebrities could use to escape the press. Signor Zilli didn't, so at some point everyone knew that George would have to face them. So what did he do? He put a napkin over his head, covered his makeshift bandana with a hat and wrapped a scarf around his neck and face. He was putting on a disguise – while actually drawing even more attention to himself. The paps got the pictures, of course, and made even more of them than if they'd just had an ordinary shot of him in the street. At the time I hadn't seen the point – until I realised that this was what some stars wanted. They could play the media game and always delivered what was required to make a splash.

Naomi Campbell is someone else who has a bizarre relationship with the cameras – the same cameras that have made her rich and famous. One time I was sitting in our sunny window table on Dean Street when she arrived for lunch. She parked the car opposite, crossed the road on the way to our bar and then one of my customers took a picture of her. Her mood changed instantly. She stormed in and demanded that I take the customer's camera and smash it for her. Fortunately, in the end we sorted it out without having to go quite so far. It was quite a while before I saw Naomi again – though I do have a great memory of her tucking into a plate of suckling pig at one private party, which makes a change from the standard-issue lettuce leaf you expect to serve most supermodels.

Harvey Keitel lived his public life in a completely different way. I thought he was a god and I put *Mean Streets* and *Taxi Driver* up among my all-time favourite films. I was thrilled when he first came to Signor Zilli for lunch. I was beside myself when he came again the next day. I was overcome when he turned into a regular.

What Harvey liked to do was sit outside and soak up the sun, just like me. That meant he had to be in our window or on one of the tables we squeezed on to the edge of the Soho pavement. Sitting there meant he could hardly avoid the autograph hunters, let alone the photographers. But he never cared. He would sign away, even if a queue of fans formed, snaking down Dean Street. He proved he was a gentleman.

With so much star power in my restaurant, I suppose I can be excused for temporarily taking my eye off the ball when it came to the money. I loved having my new self-contained, totally private party room underneath the Soho streets at Signor Zilli, so I would throw invites around like confetti. I'd be at a club with a great crowd; we'd be drinking, dancing, partying and then someone would say they were hungry.

'Come back to mine. I'll cook for you!' I'd say, night

after bleeding night. And so I did, cooking up vast pots of pasta, mixing up big salads, opening the wine fridge and making all the same mistakes I had made at Maynards. I love the Las Vegas tourist slogan – what happens in Vegas stays in Vegas. People felt that what happened in Signor Zilli stayed in Signor Zilli. Everything except my stock and my profits. Why was it taking me so long to learn from my own mistakes?

The end result was that a year after getting my name above the door I was running what felt to me like the hottest restaurant in town. I was taking thousands of pounds a day – and once more I was in danger of losing everything. It felt ridiculous, because this should have been such a good time. On any given lunchtime, I could have supermodels and actors upstairs having a great time with their friends. Then I could have what felt like the entire cast of *EastEnders* and most of Spandau Ballet all eating late-night or early-morning pasta in my family room downstairs.

But despite all this, I had the banks on my back and I hated it. I was running a big overdraft for the first time in my life. My parents had never had any money to their name, but they had never owed any either. I hated the feeling of having debts. I could lose out myself, but I didn't want to drag anyone down with me, not even my bank manager. More importantly, I didn't want to drag David Austin down. I wouldn't have got Signor Zilli open without his cash. It was money he had lent to me on a handshake and money I swore I would repay. But, as the cash poured out of the business, I had to face the fact that I was stuck.

In the end, Italy saved me – or, more specifically, an apartment that I had bought there back in the early days of Il Siciliano. I managed to sell it fast. But the nightmare wasn't quite over. Day after day, I had to work on the books, squeeze out extra cash and fine-tune the business. I learned some great lessons about management. I learned I could survive just about anything. But, after it all, I was ready for a bit of a break and I decided to have some fun. I flew over to Holland to hang out with George Michael on his Faith tour. It was time for another party.

CHAPTER THIRTEEN

Running Away

Going on tour with George was like entering a high-pressure, always-on, utterly crowded underground world. So many people are involved in keeping his show on the road. So many men and women dressed in black, carrying clipboards and barking instructions into walkie talkies the moment we passed them.

George was performing at the Rotterdam Arena and we were staying at a slick, fancy hotel in Amsterdam.

George was full of energy on that tour and his voice was strong and pitch perfect. The concert had sold out, of course, and at the end the fans were determined to keep calling him back to the stage. When he finally left, there was a mad dash through the arena corridors and out to the tour bus.

Every second counts because you are desperate to be on the road before the real crowds arrive. We were laughing like kids as we bundled on board and yelled at the driver to move. George knew he had done a great

143

show and was still on a massive high. He was sweating like no one I had ever seen. We switched seats halfway through the journey so George could get away from the window and I soaked my own shirt through to my skin with the sweat he had left behind.

Our nights out in Amsterdam were wild. We made a weekend of it. Or maybe it was a week – it felt like it. After George's concerts, we hit the town in a big way. George was still years away from officially coming out of the closet. But behind the scenes his sexuality wasn't exactly a big secret. The clubs we went to said it all.

The first one we all poured into was pumping with music, reeking of smoke and booze and packed out. Packed out with dozens and dozens of men, that is. I'm looking for the women, trying to see if there's at least a few of them about to join the dance floor. Then I saw two guys kissing. Kissing as if their lives depended on it. I sighed a little bit. There wasn't going to be anything here for me. But at least I knew we would be on the move soon. With George we always were. It was a case of swing into the bar, grab drinks, sink them fast then swing on. So in no time at all we were out in the Amsterdam streets and on the move.

'That wasn't exactly my scene,' I joked to the gang as we headed off. 'Can't we find somewhere a bit more mixed so we can all have fun?'

But next time was the same. More men. More kissing.

This set the pattern for the whole night. We never stopped anywhere for long. Sweep in. Get drinks. Move around. Sweep out. Move on. George was always hyper after his concerts – couldn't sit or stand still.

Travelling with George wasn't like travelling with anyone else – not least because it was only George who got asked for autographs at immigration and passport control. But in France, he found out that no matter how famous you are, if Parisians say 'non', they mean 'non'. We were going to Paris for the most ridiculous of reasons. David had an apartment there and had just bought a new dining-room table. He wanted us to come over and see it. As it turned out, David was so late getting to the airport that he nearly missed the plane himself. But half a dozen of us got together in a bistro in Paris for a long lunch on our first day and then decided to flag down a taxi to get over to his apartment. None would stop for us. The more cabs we tried to hail, the more we got rejected. George tried to persuade some of the drivers that he would tip big. But they just didn't like the look of us. Too big a group, one told us. But for some reason, we didn't think to split into two groups of three. We were on a group trip. We wanted to stick together.

So, on a blindingly hot day, we all started the hike across the parks and boulevards of Paris to David's apartment. We were a little bit pissed, sweating like pigs and got seriously lost within the hour. And why? Because George Michael, the world's biggest solo recording star, was unable to flag down a single French cab driver.

Back in London, I knew I would soon have to face up to my money problems. I'd paid the bill the night before in a champagne bar in Paris, because I was the only one in the group who had remembered to take my credit card. How the hell had we drunk that much? If I charged that kind of mark-up for booze back in Signor Zilli, I'd be a bleeding millionaire.

One of the many reasons I wasn't a millionaire was because I always seemed to be first to pay the bill whenever I was out with a group of people. It was somehow ingrained in me to offer, probably because even when I was a success I was terrified that people might think I was poor. In particular, I didn't want George to think I was still that peasant boy from Italy. I wanted him to know I was a successful restaurant owner in London. So I overcompensated on everything. With him, with the entourages, with all our other friends and hangers-on. And then I worried about money even more, constantly doing all the old sums in my head to see if I could make it through another week, month or year.

I think money problems can probably cause people as much pain as health problems. Worrying about money can destroy relationships because it just eats away at you from the moment you wake up to the moment you go to bed. It gets into your dreams as well. They turn into nightmares. You start to resent every penny your partner spends when times are tough – even if you're spending far more than they are. Then they start resenting you. And so the downward spirals begin. Looking back, I reckon my own marriage was about to become the best ever example of that.

The weird thing is that you can have the worst money worries of your life just as you enjoy the best times. I had been out clubbing with some other Italians and we'd had a bit of a laugh with a group of Madonna's dancers over at Browns. They had then invited us to join them all for dinner at the Waldorf Hotel the next evening. A bit posh for a bunch of hard-up dancers, I thought. But maybe Madonna pays great wages. Even if she didn't, I had been a master of living beyond my means when I was their age. I guessed their plan was to nurse a single drink all evening while they tried to look as if they fitted in. I liked that 'fake it till you make it' attitude, so I was very happy to play along.

Anyway, it turned out there was more to our dinner at the Waldorf than a cheap drink and an early exit. The minute we arrived, we were led to a roped-off area of the dining room and shown a big round table. A big round table where I sat next to Nick Kamen and Madonna herself. At that point, Nick was the hottest male star in town, having stripped off in his Levi's advert and launched a singing career on the back of his fame. Madonna was simply the hottest female star in the world.

To my embarrassment, I became tongue-tied. I could talk to anyone when I had big names in my restaurant, on my turf. I was in control there and I had the confidence that came from being the host. Here I was just a short Italian that neither of them had heard of. I felt like a nobody and I was terrified that it would show. So what would I say to Madonna? How do you start a conversation with the Queen of Pop?

I picked a bad way. I was convinced that her family were originally from my region of Italy in Abruzzo. It was my opening gambit. 'I'm from the same place as you!' I began.

'What? America?' she replied, turning away.

My opening line turned into my final line and our conversation seemed over.

To be fair to her, Madonna did have other things on her mind that night. Well, one thing: Nick Kamen. I was pretty much ignored as some high-octane flirting went on across me. It took the pressure off, to be honest. And it was as I sat back and tried to look relaxed that I spotted George and Andros come into the dining room. They both waved and smiled and headed over to say hello and join us.

But the Waldorf security staff stopped them in their tracks. George Michael wasn't allowed across the velvet rope to speak to Aldo Zilli for quite some time. The world had gone mad! I don't think I've ever enjoyed giving a big shrug as much as I did that night. 'Sorry, what can I do?' I wanted it to say. 'I'm a bit busy with my friends, right now. Call me later. Gotta go.' Then I tried to look as if Madonna's shameless flirting was aimed at me and was the most fascinating thing I had ever seen.

Jack Nicholson was the next superstar I met – and once again it all got a bit confusing. I'd gone dancing at Browns as usual and was kicking back in the private VIP room upstairs. Jack walked in just as the girl I was chatting to got up to go to the ladies room. She knew him, introduced him to me and he sat in one of the armchairs right opposite me. I was beside myself with excitement. Jack is one of those celebrities who is exactly the same in real life as he is on film. It really is as if he is on set, playing Jack Nicholson, the famous, bad-boy actor.

Another special occasion. With Michelle Collins at her birthday party. This was also the opening night of Zilli Fish.

Above left: With Chris Evans, in the Guinness building on St. Patrick's Day, Dublin.

Above right: Another night on the town. Checking out the Soho bars with Chris.

Above left: With Denise van Outen and Donna Air filming for Sky One

Above right: With restaurant critic, A.A.Gill, winning the award for Best Italian Restaurant.

Below: Nikki at work, modelling

Above: Me and my daughter on holiday in Italy in 1999.

Below: Bonding with my daughter, Laura, in 1995, on one of our many holidays in Italy.

Above left: With Chris Tarrant during filming of *Celebrity X-Factor*.

Above right: With little Billie Piper.

Below: With my good friend, Patsy Palmer.

Me and Nikki on our wonderful wedding day.

Above left: Cheers!

Above right: Fishing on a Greek island

Below: My little son Rocco and me.

Nikki, Rocco and me.

courtesy of www.chrisbracewell.com

And, whatever age he was then, it was clear that he still had an incredible eye for women. He also had magnetism. They didn't just go for him because he was rich and famous. He could have got them if he'd driven a bus. Even the blokes fancied him that night at Browns.

Anyway, we got talking – me, with Jack Nicholson! I told him about my restaurant. He loved Italy and Italian food, so he wanted to know more.

'So, you got a card for this place?'

Jack Nicholson wanted to come to my restaurant! But no, I didn't have a card.

'I'll go and write it all down for you.'

I threw myself across the room, dived at the bar, begged the waiter for a pen and paper and wrote out Signor Zilli's address. By the time I had got back to my table, Jack had moved on. Seems people like Jack always do move on. But, if anyone reading this can get a message to him, do please say I'd love to finally cook him that true Italian meal. And that now I even carry cards to the bathroom, just in case I might need them.

CHAPTER FOURTEEN

Royalty

For the next few weeks, I walked around on a high after my brief connection with Hollywood royalty. I kept hoping Jack might track me down. He does that kind of thing in films. But it turned out it didn't matter. I was about to meet some real royalty instead. Signor Zilli is in the heart of London's theatreland, and that's where Prince Edward was working after leaving the marines.

He had a job with Andrew Lloyd Webber's Really Useful Group, who were all regular lunch and dinner guests. The first I knew that Prince Edward might join them one day came when we had a visit from his royal protection officers. I had a rough idea that the police probably checked out places the royal family visited, but I'd never really thought through what it might entail. Did they sweep for angles where snipers might be posted on nearby rooftops? A safe room to escape a bomb? A street that can be closed off after a kidnap attempt?

As it turns out, it didn't seem as James Bond as all

that. They mainly check the fire exits, the fire alarms and the smoke detectors. So, if you want to avoid being burned alive, pick restaurants that attract royalty – you'll know everything will be in full working order. The Prince then turned up a few days later – and I nearly missed him altogether. He was with around half a dozen colleagues and really was just one of the gang. He was posh, but couldn't have been more ordinary. I liked him.

A few weeks later, he came by again, with a smaller group. And then he came on a date with the singer Ruthie Henshall. They couldn't have been more together and again they couldn't have been more ordinary – though the bodyguard who had to sit with them all night did sort of set them apart from most other courting couples. I felt sorry for that guy, the ultimate gooseberry, but hopefully he was well paid. We tried to feed him well, though he wasn't allowed to drink.

Edward and Ruthie became regular guests and as such they got special treatment. She was in shows such as *Les Mis* and *Miss Saigon* at the time, so couldn't arrive until very late. He was often checking out other shows for Really Useful, so they met at Signor Zilli just before midnight. The night I nearly got my head chopped off by royal decree came when they had another romantic night upstairs and I had a party downstairs with a group of my mates.

'Stay up here with them and let me know if they need anything,' I told one of my waiters. 'I'll make it worth your while in the morning.' I walked over to Edward and Ruthie. 'I'll be downstairs and we'll try to keep the noise down,' I joked.

'Thanks, Aldo, we'll be fine,' Edward said. They looked it.

A couple of hours passed and without me knowing my waiter decided to bugger off home. He said goodbye to Edward and Ruthie but didn't tell me. Downstairs I'd had a few drinks and we had all started to talk about the royal family. At exactly the wrong time. I was mouthing off about how much I fancied Princess Diana and why she would be so much better off with a red-blooded Italian man rather than a stuffed shirt of a British prince when I felt a tap on my shoulder…

'Aldo, you've locked us in,'

It was Edward, being a gentleman by ignoring my very loud commentary on his older brother.

I got Edward and Ruthie their coats, unlocked the door and waved them goodbye. Then I fell about laughing with the boys from downstairs. But Edward wasn't done with us yet. Somehow, I heard banging on the door above the sound of our party. I headed back up and there he was.

'You've given me the wrong coat, Aldo,' he said.

'Sorry – again,' was all I could say this time. I found his coat and handed it to him. Then as he headed away with a smile I booted out all my friends and tried to sober up in case bad things really do happen in threes. I wanted to be ready in case Edward came back after yet another problem.

As the 1980s headed to a close, Signor Zilli finally turned the corner, and we hit the 1990s in pretty good shape. I was much more careful about how I ran things now. If you want a restaurant to succeed, you need to remember that it's a business. You need to be professional and pay attention to the details, right down to the number of loo rolls your supposedly rich celebrity diners will pinch from the customer toilets. Shame on you, all the women with the stuffed handbags and the men with something under their coats. I watched the stock coming in, the leftovers going out and constantly readjusted our meals so we offered exactly what people wanted at exactly the right prices.

I enjoyed being in control of everything – carrying so many details in my head, just as my dad had done on the farm a lifetime ago. After such a rocky start, I knew I couldn't lose Signor Zilli. It meant too much to me, I was having too much fun and I was still making too many new friends.

Paul and Stacey Young were great – they were among the first to arrive for a party someone was throwing at Signor Zilli one night and they actually helped the staff get the room ready, which made me like them from the start. They then introduced me to another lifelong friend, Michelle Collins. We met at a club called Quiet Storm and as a new star of *EastEnders* Michelle was the centre of everyone's attention. But she was no prima donna.

She came in to Signor Zilli for dinner shortly afterwards and we talked properly. She was genuine, hard-working and kind. I liked her – and I liked joining the soap opera of her life. Fortunately, we never crossed the line in our relationship – which has, I think, made it stronger. It's still strong today and she is the godmother to my son.

Today I go to her house for New Year's Eve parties and she is so obviously just the same Michelle Collins she was as a girl. She's never bought into the celebrity world. There can be a hundred people at her party and not one of them will be anything other than a genuine friend.

Michelle was always the first to take the piss out of me about the way I looked. I had a ponytail and she always wanted to sneak up behind me with a pair of scissors and chop it off. Other people took the mickey about the clothes I wore. I couldn't have cared less. Clothes mattered to me. They still do. When my family told me I had failed because I came back from my first winter in Germany in the same hand-me-down trousers, I took it to heart. Very rich people with very old money can be relaxed about what they wear and what they have. People who have fought for everything need to find a way to show it all off. I needed to find a way to prove I was a success and clothes were the first thing I thought of. I wanted to create good first impressions. I wanted to be noticed and remembered.

When you are Signor Zilli, you are your own best advertisement and I knew I had to keep it fresh. And what the hell: I like big, bright, colourful clothes. London can be a grim, hard, grey city. What's so wrong with a splash of colour if it makes people smile?

With all that in mind, I suppose it was obvious I'd go for some brilliant Versace clothes. And when I got the chance to meet the man himself, I jumped at it. Trouble was I don't think I could have acted less cool if I had tried.

It was 1992 and Gianni Versace was in London to open his vast, five-storey shop on Bond Street. Try as I might, I couldn't get him to eat with me at Signor Zilli. But I did bag myself an invite to his opening-night party. The paparazzi and the crowds outside the store were incredible – they made the modest groups of snappers we'd get on Dean Street look positively pathetic. Much of the excitement came because of a rumour that Princess Diana might show up. Back then, she was the ultimate draw. Like every other Soho restaurant owner, I was frustrated that she would never lunch east of Knightsbridge. I even dreamed of opening a Zilli West near Harrods just so I could meet her. I would have happily shut the place down the next day having fulfilled the ambition.

Back on Bond Street for Gianni's party, I knew the press didn't really want to take my picture. I was hardly in the A-list, but I was still loving it. I was there with PR guru Neil Reading and I posed and pouted on that red carpet, whether the press was interested or not. It was ages before I could be persuaded to actually go into the shop itself. When I did, I entered an equally mad world. Straight away, I got lucky – and poor Gianni got an irritating new 'friend'.

Somehow, I ended up in the same lift as Gianni and some of his real friends as we all headed up to the main party floor, where George Michael and Elton John were hosting a private event. I can't remember if Gianni and I actually spoke as we headed up. But I do remember that I glued myself to the poor man for the rest of the night. Whoever he talked to, wherever he went, however much he moved around the rooms, Gianni would turn around and find I was still there, at his left shoulder, grinning away, sticking my face forward and acting like the back end of a pantomime horse. I even got calls from friends halfway through the night because I was live on *News at Ten*. They had been filming the party and there I was, apparently, right alongside Gianni, George Michael and Elton John. Every picture taken of Gianni on his big night, there I was: leering at the camera, glassy eyed and thinking I was the coolest cat in town. Fortunately for Gianni, he never had to go to the loo, because I'm sure I'd have shadowed him there as well.

The mad excess of the Versace-store days summed up the early part of the 1990s. There was a spend, spend, spend mentality going on, and for once a lot of that cash was being spent in my restaurant. The optimist and the party animal in me were loving it – convinced it would last forever. The worrier and the businessman in me told a different story. Unfortunately, this half of me would turn out to be right.

The first Gulf War of the early 1990s cast a long shadow in London. Whenever bombs start dropping, every restaurant and club owner feels the effect. The tourist market takes an immediate dive and Desert Storm had made the locals in London feel too worried to go out and have fun as well. When businesses stop entertaining at lunch and dinner, things get really serious. And they had stopped almost overnight this time around.

Our takings at Signor Zilli had gone through the floor and were still refusing to pick back up. I had a lot of sleepless nights back then because I had been hoping to finally repay my debt to David Austin. Now all my money was disappearing just by keeping Dean Street in business. I needed more time from David and I offered him the deeds to my Italian house as an act of faith. In an act of friendship, he said no.

So, as the world stayed serious I knew I had to follow suit. I knuckled down again. When one or two of our staff left that spring, we didn't replace them. Everyone just worked a whole lot harder. I was back in the kitchen every day, back at the markets every morning, back on the books every night. My nights on the town and the blagging I did to get on the red carpet and film premieres and into the best clubs all ended.

Our skeleton crew scraped and scratched our way through the really quiet patches, covering our costs by the skin of our teeth. And in the process I learned something I should have already known. Famous-name clients were wonderful and made my restaurant unique. But it was everyone else who made the real difference. I needed my regulars to see me through. I wanted the local residents and the workers who would turn up in good times and bad. I needed the out-of-towners who came up for a special occasion once a year but made the most of every second they were in town. Like David, all these people were real friends. And some of them could spring some real surprises.

One example came on a bizarre day when the economy and the news headlines were still grim but Signor Zilli was somehow buzzing. Most restaurants were half-empty and my upstairs room was nowhere near full. But the few guests I did have were about as high profile as it was possible to be. A hotshot new actor called Matt Damon was in town. Apparently, someone in America had told him about this Italian man with a Soho restaurant, so he was sitting there with some friends. It was well before *Good Will Hunting* and no one really knew who Matt was, but everyone said he would be famous one day. They were right and he certainly got a lot of admiring glances from all the ladies who were lunching that day. One of my waiters couldn't take his eyes off him either.

Meanwhile, Naomi Campbell must have forgotten about the incident with the photographer because she was holding court on a table near by. Liz Hurley, my ultimate posh tall English fantasy figure, was there, and Prince Edward was part of a big Really Useful group at the back of the room.

But, for all this glamour and excitement, it was an anonymous-looking Greek guy who would mean the most to me that lunchtime. He had been in a few times before and was on his way to becoming a regular, though as yet I knew very little about him. The staff cuts meant I was spending a lot more time in the kitchen rather than front-of-house, but, when I was serving some food and checking on the room, he mouthed a question.

'Can I have a word, please, when it's quiet?'

'Certainly.'

I went back to the kitchens feeling just a little nervous. With a supermodel, an actress, Hollywood royalty and real royalty in the room I couldn't afford to have some guy trying to create a scene. I didn't want him to try to show off with some made-up complaint. We'd had enough trouble with people like that already. A while ago, a couple had complained about finding a hair in their meal. We'd knocked something off their bill. A week later, the same couple reported a piece of glass in some pasta. Free dinner. Third time, they produced a screw that they said had been on their plate. But this time one of my waiters had seen them put it there themselves. They were out faster than you could say 'screw you'.

Please don't let this guy be a trouble-maker like that, I thought. It turned out that I needn't have worried. This man was going to set a chain of events in motion that would save – not harm – my business.

'Good crowd today. You certainly know how to pull in the names.' This strange Greek man had joined me at the bar after his meal.

Our celebrity friends had all left, Prince Edward patting me on the shoulder as usual as he passed, his security man giving me a simple nod and a smile. Even Naomi had been in a good mood that day, throwing plenty of kisses around as she made her big exit.

'It's been good. Everyone seems to have enjoyed themselves.'

'You must be coining in the money.'

'We do OK,' I lied. If only he knew.

'I own a club,' he said, clearly having decided the time for small talk was over. 'Ascot, on Green Street. It needs this kind of atmosphere. It needs those kinds of clients. I want you to come and take a look at it.'

'You want me to buy it?' I don't know why I thought that, but I couldn't work out what else this man might be getting at.

He laughed. 'No. It's mine and I'm not selling. Just take a look. I need a consultancy. If you agree to run it for me, I'll pay you £1,000 a week, in cash. If you can turn it around, we'll talk more. If not, then we'll just leave it. No pressure either way. You want to give it a try?'

I excused myself, saying I needed to go for a pee while I thought about it. I told him I wasn't sure about fitting the job in. What a laugh. As I stood looking at myself in the mirror of our upstairs toilet, I was almost shaking. A thousand pounds cash a week. For trying to perk up some dodgy Mayfair nightclub. That was a big slice of our market money right there. It could be enough to push us from the knife-edge right back into profit. And even if this gig didn't last long, it could tide us over until business really recovered, which I knew it would. This was exactly – *exactly* – what I needed. Like hell I wanted time to think about it.

'I'd love to come and take a look at your club,' I said when I got back to the bar, no longer playing hard to get. And, like almost every other important deal I have ever done, we shook hands on it.

Ascot was a typical English members club. It had deep, rich carpets, solid old furniture, heavy patterned wallpaper. The words 'faded glory' summed it up perfectly. Stuffy old English colonels might want a place that felt as if the world hadn't changed and where the Brits still ran an empire. But I could see why a pushy new Greek owner might want a revamp. A sexy, confident-looking lady called Diana Louca was running the place and was clearly suspicious of me from the start. But there was something in her eye the first time I met her. Maybe there was something in mine too. I think we both realised we were never going to be rivals. We would be colleagues. We could be friends. I told her, straight up, that I wasn't going to try and undermine her.

'I just want to make your life easier,' I told her.

'I just want to collect my £1,000 cash a week,' was what I was thinking.

And so we set to work. Diana was great with people and we both tried to lighten up the look and feel of the club. I tried to get it talked about and drag over some famous friends. It would never be Aspinalls or Tramp or Browns. But we were pulling it into the 20th century and we were enjoying it.

I liked the challenge and I loved my consultancy cash. Just as I had predicted, it came at exactly the right time. Memories of the Gulf War had finally faded and by the summer of 1992 the world seemed to be back to normal. Best of all, everyone's purse strings were loosening again. Signor Zilli was full, upstairs and down. We had ridden out the storm, though several of my restaurant friends had not been so lucky. I watched as other places shut up shop because recovery came too late for them. For me, the difference between success and failure had relied on a single conversation at lunch from a customer I had barely known.

Funnily enough, I was about to learn an important lesson from my other Greek friend that year. George Michael's life was going to go from some extreme highs to some awful lows. He was going to teach me how important it was to have a soulmate on your side.

We were still part of a loose group of friends and family who hung out together and enjoyed life. One big night we all got tickets for the Freddie Mercury Tribute Concert at Wembley. Beforehand, we met up at George's cousin's house up in North London. I was trying to be upbeat about the concert, even though I knew it was in memory of a much-loved lost friend. But it turned out I was being too loud.

'Keep the noise down. George's boyfriend is sleeping next door,' Andros told me.

It was pretty much the first time anyone had said out loud that George was gay. More interestingly, he had a boyfriend. I couldn't wait to meet him. The man in question was Anselmo Feleppa. He was just the kind of good man George deserved.

But seeing George in the good times with Anselmo forced me to think about my own marriage. Did I have a soulmate, like George? I'd married so young and had changed a lot. Deep down I knew I had to do something about it. But it would be years before I could bring myself to take a really close look at my marriage.

As always happened back then, I always focused on my business whenever personal issues needed attention. My priorities were all wrong and I would ultimately pay dearly for it. But the restaurant wasn't exactly an easy partner itself. The money from my nightclub-owning benefactor had saved me. But, as ever, things would never be this simple. Before I could properly thank my friend, he was gone. Less than a year after I started working for Ascot, he was shot dead in Leicester Square.

To this day, Diana and I know next to nothing about the incident. We don't know who killed him, or why. The police didn't say if he was the intended victim or a man in the wrong place at the wrong time. To be honest, I don't really know who he was in the first place. But the money and the experience he gave me at Ascot saved my business. And even in death his influence was far from over.

Diana walked into Signor Zilli one afternoon less than a year later. We had stayed in touch and remained friends all along, but this wasn't a social call. She had a business proposition to discuss. 'We did well at Ascot and we enjoyed it, right?' she began as we settled down to talk about old times with a coffee.

'It was brilliant. I still can't believe it's over.'

'Well, let's start it again. I've got some money put aside. We should open a new place of our own. Together.'

The whole idea was crazy. I had barely survived a major downturn in business. I'd seen just how fickle and frightening the London market could be. I knew how easy it was to lose everything. 'Why the hell not?' I said, not even needing to pretend to have a pee while I thought it over. The optimist in me had beaten down all the sensible voices that should have been in my head. As usual, I was looking right at the future, forgetting about the past.

Diana and I had a great time talking, planning and dreaming about our new venture. She knew a huge amount about the London scene, but had been held back by the traditional nature of Ascot. And I felt I was being held back by the two narrow upstairs and downstairs rooms of Signor Zilli. Both of us wanted a new blank canvas to work on. We found it right next door.

CHAPTER FIFTEEN

The Zilli Empire

Every day I used to think how great it would be to take over the art gallery alongside me at 40 Dean Street. I didn't just want a bigger restaurant. I wanted to open London's first genuine Italian bar.

I'd had the dream ever since walking into the now legendary Bar Italia on Frith Street when I had first come to London. I ordered an espresso and I remember they had a single teaspoon attached to the bar with a string for everyone to stir their coffees. They also had the best atmosphere in town. The Puledri family had owned it for something like fifty years. I respected them hugely and over the years we became close. Bizarrely enough, Nino Puledri used to make his own wine up in Barnet, of all places. No idea quite how he did it. But he used to give me a bottle most years. I never got around to telling him it tasted like paint stripper!

As an Italian football fan, Bar Italia came to mean even more to me over the years. They show the World

167

Cup there and the atmosphere is incredible. I was in Bar Italia when Italy beat West Germany in 1982. I would be there again when they beat France in 2006. So, while I wanted to create something similar myself, I didn't want to destroy the Bar Italia magic or tread on the Puledris' toes. That's why my idea for the empty space on Dean Street was slightly different. I would focus on food and drink as much as on coffee. I felt we could do well with an easy mix of the formal and the informal. A truly social and relaxed place. You wanted a few drinks and a comfortable time with your friends or colleagues? In my Italian bar, I wanted to make sure you could have it. After a few drinks, some of you decide you want a decent meal? There's a special, simple menu for that as well. No rules, no stuffy minimum table orders or instructions to leave by a certain time. Just the kind of easygoing place everyone grows up with in Italy. I was convinced the idea could take off in London. With Diana's financial help and management skill, I could find out if I was right.

The premises were available in 1993 and our offer for them was accepted. The only bad news was that by taking over the art gallery we lost the kudos of using that as a guide to our location. 'Right next to the art gallery' always sounded wonderfully classy. Now we had spread into 40 Dean Street, we had a new next-door neighbour at number 39. 'Next door to the porn cinema' didn't have such a good ring to it! But I suppose it got us remembered. Anyway, sex shop or no sex shop we were on our way.

We definitely needed to get the look and feel of the place right. I wanted a rich English oak floor and some traditional, eye-catching colours in our tiles, ceramics and surfaces. We found some fantastic Italian craftsmen who could pretty much read my mind. Go there today to look at the floors if nothing else. It's real. It's the kind of quality nowhere else has any more. The bar was my baby and it's grown up well.

From the start, Signor Zilli Bar seemed to be full of people having a good time. Our gamble of allowing people to sit with drinks rather than forcing them to buy food had paid off. The more relaxed people felt, the more they seemed to spend. Sometimes we served as many food covers in the bar as we did in Signor Zilli next door.

Working out the menu for the bar was refreshing in itself. I love designing new dishes. Our challenge was to keep it simple, make sure we could serve food relatively quickly and cater for people who fancied a few nibbles as well as those who wanted pretty much the full monty. I liked mixing up my childhood favourites with some British surprises.

Today we've still got things like fish and chips alongside the grilled tunas and king prawns. I knew pizzas would be popular and if we had had a bit more money and a lot more space I wanted a traditional wood-burning oven to cook them in. As it turned out, I would have to wait a few more years to get one of those. So, at Signor Zilli Bar, I tried to at least make our pizzas a bit different. We were among the first to put rocket and parma ham, and roasted Mediterranean vegetables and goat's cheese, on our pizzas. We couldn't make them fast enough.

Risottos were still popular – although they had been such a gamble when I'd put them on my first menus in Il Siciliano. Now there are saffron, spinach and prawn risottos alongside our traditional seafood and mushroom versions. We came up with some great Italian desserts and I found some fantastic Italian coffee to serve. I'm proud to say it all worked. The money poured in and when Diana wanted to cash up her stake a year or so later, I was able to pay her with a smile. Our joint adventure had been wonderful. And all because of a strange Greek guy we never properly knew!

Building up Signor Zilli Bar had given me a taste for expansion. I wasn't alone. It was the 1990s, and London's restaurant scene was being transformed yet again. The super chef had arrived; the celebrity chef wasn't far behind. I didn't want to be left in everyone's wake. When I took over 40 Dean Street I had proudly added a further couple of dozen covers to my empire, but Terence Conran certainly upstaged me. He edged just a little ahead by opening Quaglino's, which could seat 300 diners with over 100 more drinkers at his bar. Two years later, in 1995, he moved one street away from us over on Wardour Street. And he did it in a huge way. Mezzo had something like 600 seats for diners with room for 150 drinkers in its bars, with more than 100 covers just across Soho at the new Atlantic Bar & Grill. It was clear that big was beautiful. I decided it was time I caught up.

I did a lot of walking around, looking in other restaurant windows, examining their menus and trying to keep ahead of all the trends. All restaurant owners do this. I remember when a young Gordon Ramsay was working at Aubergine, I spotted him outside Signor Zilli taking notes from our menu board. I grabbed an actual menu to give him as a joke, but by the time I got outside he'd disappeared.

Anyway, when I was pounding the streets in the second half of the 1990s I spotted one place that I was convinced could have my Zilli name written all over it. The whole block between Lexington Street and Great Pulteney Street on Brewer Street in Soho had been boarded up for as long as I could remember. It wasn't exactly the cutting edge of town, despite the arrival of the Atlantic on nearby Glasshouse Street. And I was a bit worried it might be a stretch for well-heeled London diners.

Raymond's Revue Bar was practically next door and a lot of very friendly ladies would greet any single men walking around. Apparently, you could always have a good time if you just followed them down into their basement bars. On ground level, things weren't much better. Sex was starting to sell well in Soho and plenty of dodgy shops were opening up on and around Brewer Street as well. If I did get a restaurant there, I thought I would probably have to give up on my dream of ever getting Princess Diana to lunch there. There was no mistaking this part of town for Knightsbridge.

Anyway, as I walked around I was convinced that the sad old site on Brewer Street deserved a second chance at life. And I was lucky that Soho was still a village. I had become part of its secret, close-knit little community and I knew all the elders. I found out who owned that boarded-up part of our manor, I paid him a visit and we did a deal – which involved me turning around the menus and kitchen of a pub he owned near by.

Back on Brewer Street I was thinking hard. I was never going to have a 600-seat mega-restaurant, but I wanted to make waves all the same. I had a plan for something very new. I just hoped London was ready for it.

Nino and I talked long and hard about my idea, and I took advice from a lot of others as well. But, in the end, I knew I had to follow my instincts. I wanted to run London's very best fish restaurant.

I always remember how shocked I was when I first started working in my hot basement kitchens in London at nineteen years of age. Where were the fish on any of the menus? We had served more, much more, back in Munich, which isn't exactly coastal. Why were Londoners so scared of eating some of the freshest and healthiest food around? When they ate fish, why was it always deep-fried or covered in some rich, sickly sauces?

Over the following decade, Britain had shown signs of catching up. The message was getting through that fish was good for you. Vegetarians weren't being laughed at as much – though some chefs who can remain nameless still did so. People were worrying about heart disease, finding out about cholesterol and being turned off by horror stories about how cows, chickens and pigs were treated in factory farms. Fish had to be the answer to all of this. But could a restaurant that didn't sell anything else really make it?

Some posh places had made a go of it. But could I do

it with somewhere popular? What the hell. If you're going to gamble, then gamble big. I was going to go for it. I was going to put my name over another door. I stuck to my upside down, long-lettered logo, though this time I dotted the 'i's with sea shells. Then I added the key new word: fish. Job done, Zilli Fish was ready to be born. To any women who say that men don't understand the pain of childbirth, I offer the pain of opening a new restaurant. It's hell. And by 1997 it was all the more intense, because the rules and regulations had toughened up dramatically since I'd opened Signor Zilli nearly a decade earlier. There were so many more legal requirements to consider. Everything was getting so much more expensive, but at least our site was relatively manageable. I thanked my lucky stars I hadn't gone super-sized, like everyone else in the 1990s. I spent around £200,000 on our new place on Brewer Street. That might seem small change in today's mega-restaurant world, but it was a fortune back then. Ironically enough, most of the money went on designing something that looked incredibly simple.

We wanted a bright, clean, nice-looking room. No extras, no frills, nothing heavy or distracting. As a boy from sunny Italy, I'd always been obsessed by light. One of the things that had attracted me to the east side of Dean Street and Signor Zilli was the fact that it got so much sun in the afternoons. With the Zilli Fish site, we were mainly north facing and got less direct sunlight. So I knew we had to make the most of what there was. We went for big glass windows, wide open spaces, mirrored back walls. I didn't want people to feel down when they ate with me. I wanted them to feel as if they were on holiday. I wanted them to have fun.

The other big gamble with Zilli Fish was the position of the kitchen. Back then, most chefs still lived subterranean lives – they couldn't see their customers and the customers couldn't see them. But I remembered the relaxed Italian restaurants of my childhood where the chefs were always popping their heads around corners and diners were shown some of the theatricality of food. So we put our new kitchen right next to the dining room on Brewer Street.

Our cooks can bang, crash and curse away and it's going to add to the drama of the meal, I thought. Eating out shouldn't be about a hushed state of perfection. It should be like real life, full of real personalities. So, of course, we also had real problems and made some real mistakes. We had to stop the rebuilding work for a couple of days and risked putting back our opening night because Michael Caine was recording some film voice-overs in an underground studio next door. Our banging was being picked up by the microphones, they told us. Shame he didn't come to the opening to say thanks.

The real disaster came on our big night. To emphasise the fish just a little bit more, we had constructed a huge tropical tank to line almost the whole of the wall between the kitchen and dining room. It looked spectacular and for opening night we filled it with thirty live lobsters. I thought they would catch customers' eyes and see us through several weeks of service.

But it went wrong.

Were they warm-water lobsters or cold-water lobsters? The people filling the tank didn't ask and I didn't think to check. They got it wrong and the lobster massacre had begun by the time our first punters arrived.

'It's a fish graveyard, it looks like a fucking morgue!'

I was beside myself as we saw the dead bodies steadily mount up. The press were coming (I hoped) and I had long since worked out how they worked. I was writing headlines in my mind about us going belly up, sinking like a stone, dead lobsters and dead parrots. I could just imagine it if some famous name got sick looking at the corpses.

As our big opening approached, I just didn't know what to do – until I remembered the whole point of Zilli Fish was to keep things simple. So I knew a simple solution would save us.

We created something extra to go on the menu that night: spaghetti with fresh lobster. In my shiny new kitchen that day, it was as if I was back in Italy. I was a boy again, Mum at my side, making something up on the spur of the moment. We were using our instinct to work the flavours and make the most of what we had. My mother had only ever seen me struggle in life. She had seen me leave Italy in one set of raggedy clothes and return in the same ones. She had seen me to go to jail. She had seen me struggle for every bit of money I ever had.

That night in Soho, I think my mamma was with me. I think she saw my triumph. Spaghetti with fresh lobster was so simple – just the obvious ingredients with some extra virgin olive oil, garlic, fresh chilli, wine, tomato sauce and cherry tomatoes. But the meal was an immediate hit and it endures today. It's my signature dish, if I've got one – though, in fact, it's really my mother's.

Best of all about the Zilli Fish opening night was the mix of people drinking in the atmosphere. We had big names – which the press loved – but I had family and close friends there as well. I'd tried really hard to make sure as many of the Soho locals knew about the opening and were able to join us. I still saw Soho as my little Italian-style village in the middle of the City. So I wanted the other businesspeople to join me; I wanted the local shopkeepers and stallholders, the office staff and the residents to all feel welcome. They were. And we all had a blast.

Next day, though, it was business as usual. The razzamatazz of opening a restaurant can only last so long. It's the regular customers, the locals and the loyal fans, who really make or break you. They don't care that you had a big party the night before. They want a great meal today – that's what they're paying for. Fortunately, I was fizzing with energy at Zilli Fish.

Every day we created our menu from scratch again, just like I had at the beginning. Today, we still buy fresh every morning and then decide what to do with it. It's a bit different to the way a lot of restaurants were when I first arrived in Britain. Back then, the 'specials' boards were a real hazard to health! Chefs joke that restaurants are the most eco-friendly places around because they recycled everything. But do you really want your beef or chicken or fish being recycled?

The bad specials boards were where the results of this ingenuity got displayed. The old food they hadn't been able to sell all week was camouflaged in sauces and stews and given one last chance. Not nice. At Zilli Fish, the day's specials are just that. They're what we come up with when we see what's come fresh through the doors that morning. It's hard work but it's fun, and it's why I love being in the business.

Customers seemed to love it too. We had the buzz I had dreamed of in our big, light dining room and I could dart in and out of the kitchen all the time. No dumb waiters. No narrow flights of stairs to navigate. No risk of my missing a single trick. I could speak to all our customers and still be part of almost every meal. It worked: I'd introduced a whole new era of light Italian food and proved there was a massive market for it. We were a huge hit. In a good week back then, Zilli Fish could turn over £50,000. We started paying off our set-up costs in a little over six months and got the job done in around a year. This whole Zilli world is now my own, I thought, as I put all my past financial worries behind me. Other work was coming in all the time. Another customer who had become a friend was Neil Reading. He asked me to cook at Ascot that year which sounded like a real dream come true. I love the races and thought it would be wall-to-wall glamour. So I got all kitted out in my top hat and tails. Only to find out I was cooking for a vast group of *Sun* prize-winners in a car park... Still, we had a great laugh and when I did get a break I did still sneak into the races proper. I won some nice cash on Frankie Dettori. I also got into the Royal Box area somehow and got within inches of literally rubbing shoulders with the Queen.

The other powerful woman I met that day was the *Sun*'s Jane Moore. She had an idea for me. The *Sun*'s new 'Sun Woman' supplement wanted me to be its 'celebrity chef' and produce a weekly recipe for readers. Talk about a dream come true! But what sort of recipes should I include? And why, really, had I been picked? I knew that I was a big deal among the Soho set and I had done loads of press interviews, but at that stage I had no illusions about how well known I was to the public at large. So why would anyone want to know how I make soup? I suddenly realised that I could find the answer every lunch- and dinnertime in my dining rooms. My famous friends. I was already the world's biggest name-dropper and I decided to use them, shamelessly.

So I didn't just write recipes saying how to make something, I said who I had made it for. Minestrone Soup for Liz Hurley. Chargrilled Tuna with Red Peppers for Kate Moss. Spaghetti Vongole for Martin Kemp. It made me laugh – even though Liz, Kate and Martin's photos were almost always bigger than mine when the articles were printed.

Fortunately, everything was a laugh again back then. My business was sound. I was looking forward to every day, full of energy and ideas, ready to climb new mountains and just go for it. But, as it turned out, I was about to find a new and very big distraction. There was a vice that most British people grew up with, but which had been off limits in my hard-up Italian childhood: booze. Apart from my mad wine-bar years, I'd never been a heavy drinker. I could probably count the number of pubs I'd been into on two hands. Over the years, I had done most of my socialising with people like Freddie Mercury and George Michael and they were club people, not pub people. They were more likely to raise a glass of champagne than drink a pint of bitter. It meant I knew next to nothing about beer. My next best friend was going to change all that. At least for a while, everything about my life was going to get very silly and very crazy. I was about to meet Chris Evans.

CHAPTER SIXTEEN

Going Ginger

The warm, late-morning sunshine was drifting in through the windows of Signor Zilli as I sat with a coffee and watched Soho come to life. It's never been an early-morning sort of place, despite all the markets and the office workers. Our real characters rarely show themselves much before noon. Many of them don't seem to like the light at all!

At Signor Zilli, we had done our deliveries, marked up our menus, checked our reservations book and were enjoying the calm before the storm. Late morning is a wonderful part of a restaurant owner's day. Looking down Dean Street, I suddenly spotted an instantly recognisable figure. Chris Evans was walking past the Groucho Club a few doors down. He was with Danny Baker and one of his sidekicks from the show, and for all the big names I'd had in the restaurant lately I was as starstuck as hell. I'd loved the *Big Breakfast* and I thought *Don't Forget Your Toothbrush* was the funniest show on the box.

'Come in – have lunch!' I called out as the pair approached my windows.

Chris gave me one of the trademark toothy grins that I knew so well from the telly. He and Danny walked right in, sat down in my empty restaurant and said they would eat whatever I could cook them.

When they had finished eating, Danny left to go and see his family and Chris, his friend and I went next door to my bar. I think we downed some six bottles of pink champagne in the early afternoon alone – and for a while I had a sinking feeling that this was going to be another freebie that I would have to write off to experience. But it wasn't. When we did finally leave that evening, Chris didn't just pay the full bill and leave a big tip. He also bought bottles of champagne for everyone else who was in the bar at the time telling everyone that it was my birthday – it wasn't! That was the first good thing I noticed about him. He was utterly generous and he always paid in his own mad kind of way.

As we talked, Chris and I noticed we had a lot more in common than just a wild taste in clothes. We both liked to gossip. Once we started we never stopped.

My actual memory of that first afternoon and evening is a bit hazy – not surprisingly. But I remember being in a lap-dancing club at 2am. And I remember pretty much doing it all again the next day – and probably the next. Chris and I certainly seemed to get along.

He makes friends fast and I loved this mad ginger man. I loved how his eyes darted around the rooms, bulging out behind his big glasses. He was desperate not to miss a thing in case a better party or a cooler crowd were just around the corner. Chris was just like Freddie and George that way.

Fans were always coming up to talk to him, to put their arms around him, to buy him drinks. Several pints or shorts were often lined up on the bar from strangers over the course of a night. This was what was so different to the Freddie Mercury days, when we had always been given some respectful space.

His energy, stamina and the time he gave to his fans were sky high. But I soon learned that his boredom threshold was low. When he was tired of a conversation or a person, he had no worries about the social niceties of moving on. He just turned around and dropped it – while the other person was still talking, if necessary. And everyone forgave him. He was mad, manic and such good company. So he got away with it.

'Zildo, we're going on an adventure.'

Chris was a steamroller when he made a plan. There was never any question that you wouldn't come into line, possibly because there was no question that whatever crazy idea he had would be a brilliant experience. He was incredibly well connected and had no problem calling in favours. Everything had to be new, everything was about having fun.

So, when I told him I'd never drunk a pint of Guinness before, he didn't just buy me a pint. He knew my birthday was coming up, so he flew me over to Dublin, and got me checked into the hotel Bono had opened there. Then he made sure the man himself would be behind the bar to serve me my first true Irish pint. Oh, and I had to wear a bright-green Irish rugby shirt as well.

As birthdays go, this was one to remember. Bit of a shame I drank so much and got hazy on so much of it! But I won't forget hanging out with Bono. He was another hero of mine and, as the booze kicked in, I thought it was hilarious that, while Chris and I were in matching shirts, Chris and Bono both had equally wild specs. Try as I might, I couldn't get them to swap them for a photo, though.

Chris had been filming *TFI Friday* and doing his radio show on that trip. We were using part of the Guinness factory as the set. It seemed as if we were trying to drink it dry. But everyone got a masterclass in television and radio presenting while we were there. However wild he got, Chris could pull it back together when the cameras and the microphones clicked on. He was brilliant to watch. And you always knew the party wouldn't stop at the end of the show. For Chris, the party hardly ever stopped at all.

Back in London, Chris was doing his breakfast show on Virgin Radio. It meant he came off duty and was ready to party just as my day in Signor Zilli, the Zilli Bar and Zilli Fish was supposed to be kicking off. I was having too much fun to let this stop me from joining him, though. Nino was in charge in Dean Street and I had taken on a great team to run things at Zilli Fish. They all pulled far more than their weight while I played with my brash new best friend.

Chris loved to spring surprises and he loved to see people try something new. So after my celebrity-served first pint of Guinness, he persuaded me (it wasn't hard) to head off to sunny Portugal with the rest of his gang.

We stayed in an amazing hotel there and Chris hit the golf course before he even hit the bar. That showed just how keen he was on the game. I didn't join him.

'I've never been on a golf course in my life. It's an old man's game,' I said.

'Sod it. It's the best game in the world.'

'Old man's game.'

'It's the game of kings, you Italian idiot.'

And Chris had to prove it to me.

'It's for you. You'll never guess what it is.' He handed me a present on our private-plane trip back to Britain. It was heavy, about three foot long and had a small extra bit sticking out of one end. It was a golf club. 'You can use it where we're going next,' he told me.

We didn't land in London that day. Nino and the team had yet more mealtimes to manage without me. Chris had ordered a flight plan up north. I'd drunk Guinness in its home country and now he wanted me to play my first game of golf on its home turf as well. We were flying to Scotland and we were going to play at St Andrews.

Landing in Scotland in our private jet was as amazing as flying in it. Loads of private planes were queuing up to land alongside us – and a lot of egos came into play. Eddie Jordan kept us waiting in the air for a while because he pulled rank and managed to touch down first, we heard. When you are that rich, it's not just the size of your jet that matters – it's the order you get to land it in. I had a lot to learn.

A car picked us up at the airport and took us to our hotel – the incredible Gleneagles, where my room was roughly the size of my first flat up in Sudbury. It was the highest of the high life. And I was about to find out that in Chris's world there was always further to climb. Things could always get even more surreal.

Straight after checking in, I went down to the hotel shop to try to buy a new shirt. While I was there, a loved-up couple walked past. It was Michael Douglas and Catherine Zeta Jones. Other famous faces started to pop up in the rest of the hotel. 'Why the hell aren't you all having lunch in Zilli Fish?' I wanted to scream at one point. To which they might well have screamed back: 'Why the hell aren't you cooking at Zilli Fish?' Probably just as well I kept quiet.

The stars were all up in Scotland because Chris hadn't picked just any old weekend for my first stab at golf. It was the Dunhill Celebrity Challenge – and Chris had a surprise to spring and another joke to play. He told everyone I was his caddy and I tried to act the part as we headed out across the course. Dropping the bag and seeing all the clubs fall out on the first pristine green blew my cover. But we had plenty to laugh about as we knocked back a lot of smooth Scotch in the bar that night.

By the time Chris and I started living in each other's pockets, I'd actually thought I was a bit of a man of the world. I'd travelled, I spoke languages, I had uprooted and moved my whole life and set up a top business in a foreign country. I'd met a who's who of stars and made – and lost – a hell of a lot of money. But Chris, still in his thirties and almost exactly ten years younger than me, was always so many steps ahead.

The pubs, the Guinness, the golf, the red-eye flights to

go boozing in New York just because we could – there was always something he'd done that I hadn't. And I was always trying to catch up. Maybe it was something to do with the age gap. I'd always spent time with people older than me. I'd always been the youngster acting years ahead of his age. Now I was the older one who didn't seem to have lived as fast a life as he had thought. Chris and I set off sparks all the time. Psychologists would have had a field day – about both of us.

Skiing was next on Chris's list for his protégé. He couldn't believe that a forty-something Italian had never been on skis. So off we went to Zermatt on the Italian Swiss border. As usual, we did nothing by halves. My first slope looked like it was going to be the bloody Matterhorn.

'So what's a black run, Chris?' I asked, looking at the wildly complicated map as we headed up the mountain on our first day.

'It's the easiest one,' he lied, shooting off down what looked like the wall of death.

I tried to follow. Well, to be honest, I tried to stand up. But my first time on skis wasn't really a success. In the end, I had to beg one of the instructors to carry me down the mountain on his bloody shoulders. It was wildly humiliating, because he seemed to take me past every crowd of slim beautiful women on the mountain. He dropped me off – quite literally – outside the most crowded mountain restaurant. The lunchtime crush got something they'd laugh about for days. I then got plastered by starting the après-ski a little early.

Chris was actually a brilliant skier, far more stylish

than his gangly appearance would suggest. But I never got the hang of it that first trip. We partied hard in Zermatt, just as we partied everywhere we went. Not much sleep. Lots of lost hours. Doing a Formula One and spraying everyone in the bar with Don Perignon that we paid for but didn't even drink. A typical Chris Evans/Aldo Zilli weekend, all things considered.

Back in London, I rushed to the doctors with what I thought was exhaustion. They told me I was suffering from 'over-excitement'... Meanwhile, my true friend – the wonderful, long-suffering Nino – was being fantastic running Signor Zilli and all seemed well at Zilli Fish. I was busy learning just how hard a hangover can be, so every bit of help was gratefully accepted. And I had a new challenge on my hands. Chris wasn't the only one on television. For years now I had been building up a strong TV career of my own. I reckoned Chris could be my new mentor and teach me how to get up to the next level.

CHAPTER SEVENTEEN

Live on TV

It had begun a few years earlier in my restaurant. I was larking around in Brewer Street one sunny day and I invited a group of regulars over into the kitchen to watch me make part of their meal. One of them worked for a television company and it seemed as if he liked what he saw.

'You should do that on television,' he said.

'Give me my own show and I'd love to.'

'I'll give you a call.'

It took off from there and I didn't need encouraging. I know we're all supposed to be modest and act as if we don't really care about things, but the showman in me had probably been waiting all my life for someone to say I should go on TV. I'm an entertainer. I loved having an audience. That's why I'd invited that little group into my kitchen that day, after all. I was thrilled, childishly thrilled, about the thought of having a proper audience on TV.

Luckily for me, I could hardly have timed all this better. A whole new channel was being put together – the Carlton Food Network. They were looking for some figureheads to launch it and produce a series of new shows. They reckoned one of those people could be me. All I had to do was prove I had star quality. They wanted me to do a screen test.

The idea was for it to be as natural as possible, so we filmed it in the basement kitchen of Signor Zilli Bar. I thought I would be comfortable there. Fat chance. I couldn't believe how nervous I was when the day came. Cooking for the cameras stressed me out more than cooking for a hundred diners upstairs. And me, the man who hadn't been lost for words even when he struggled to speak a language, I was stunned to see how hard it was to cook and talk at the same time.

Everything worried me. I might set myself alight! I might chop my finger off! I might forget a recipe that I'd already cooked a thousand times! I might forget how to breathe! Kitchens have always been hot places, but I don't think I have ever sweated so much as I did at that first screen test. It reminded me of all those early mornings the party crowd and I had spent sobering up in the steam room at Champneys.

Brilliantly enough, the television people loved it. Maybe they saw that it was all from the heart. Maybe they just thought that things could only get better. Either way, I signed myself a deal. I did indeed launch Carlton Food Network, alongside Antony Worrall Thompson and Brian Turner. I was also commissioned for my first full series, *Perfect Pasta with Aldo Zilli*. It was serious stuff.

We filmed different dishes in different kitchens all over London. At all of them, I still worried about cooking and talking. I still sweated like a pig. On one occasion, I nearly *did* set myself on fire when I misjudged how close the oil got to the gas. But the producers seemed to love it. And I loved the television crews I worked with. I could see why Chris was so happy making his Channel Four shows. These were creative, exciting, passionate people. I was only on the very edge of their world, making a brand-new show for a brand-new channel. But I was on my way. 'I don't belong here, but I want to,' I told myself. It was just what I had said when I had first explored Soho as a kid all those years ago. I also felt I was getting some kind of affirmation or approval from the producers. They had picked me. They were sticking with me. Maybe they believed in me.

I wished my dad could have seen it.

The next most exciting part of the process for a television newcomer like me was to go into the studio's editing suite to see the footage put together into a proper programme. Something embarrassing happened that first time I saw myself on camera: I fell in love with myself. I was like a cocky teenager again. This dodgy figure on the screen wasn't the Aldo Zilli I had always known. It was a newer, better, bigger Aldo. It was who I wanted to be.

'I know Italian men are vain, but I really shouldn't fancy myself so much,' I thought that day in the editing suite. But I did fancy myself. Seeing my face on the screen changed everything. I even started to walk differently that afternoon. I headed back to Signor Zilli swaggering like John bloody Travolta in *Saturday Night Fever*. I looked at women differently. My show hadn't even been broadcast. It might never be shown and, even if it was, it might only be watched by a handful of people. But still I swaggered and still I leered at those unsuspecting girls. Looking back, it's lucky I wasn't arrested.

I had calmed down a bit by the time *Perfect Pasta* was finally shown – but only a bit. I was genuinely thrilled to have made this new leap on to television. I felt as if I was in the in-crowd at last. I felt cool. I felt the way I'd wanted to feel at fourteen, when I'd been stuck with my brothers' trousers and a part-time job that left me stinking of fish. At the show's launch party, I also got a buzz. I met my first agent, Fiona Lindsay. I didn't really know what an agent was back then, or why I might need one. But Fiona soon proved how important she was. She was working with Antony Worrall Thompson and had access to a lot of new deals. So pretty soon I found out that *Perfect Pasta* wasn't going to be my only show. I was asked back, and it felt fantastic to know I was doing something right. *Aldo's Italian Job* was my next challenge, while *Aldo and Friends* was like a dream come true. It did what it said on the tin – it let me mix work with pleasure.

With that show I cooked for mates such as Paul and Stacey Young, Bonnie Langford and the All Saints girls. The idea was to do the show in their own kitchens, though with Chris Tarrant we ended up in Richard Parks's house, for reasons I can't quite remember. But, wherever we were, we were surrounded by good pals and I was being paid lots of lovely money. Who could ask for more than that?

Having lost a bit of the John Travolta swagger and gained some experience, I'd like to say I had calmed down into the ultimate cool and professional television performer. But that wasn't true. I remained as nervous as ever. If I'd thought recording my shows for the Carlton Food Network was nerve-wracking, it was nothing to going on my first live broadcast. That was *The Vanessa Show* with Vanessa Feltz.

It was Shrove Tuesday and I'd been asked on to make, and toss, pancakes. Oh, and it was BBC1, so it would easily be my biggest and most important audience to date. 'Just stay calm, you know what you're doing, it'll be OK!' That's what I was telling myself as I began the show and talked viewers through the first steps to the perfect pancake. But why was the floor manager going nuts behind the cameras? What did all those arm and hand gestures mean? What was I doing wrong? A couple of minutes later I found out, on live national television. My pancake mix was made, my pancake was in the pan, the clock was ticking and I knew I should be ready to toss it and serve it up to Vanessa. But it just wasn't happening. I'd forgotten to turn on the gas...

I never got asked back on to Vanessa's show. But at least I think I got remembered, if only as the wild Italian who tried to cook without gas. And, funnily enough, Shrove Tuesday has turned out to be a good time for me. A few years later, I was invited to try to make a record number of pancakes on *This Morning*. Not everyone is going to want to be called 'the biggest tosser on television'... But as usual I was well up for the joke and to this day I'm still in the *Guinness Book of Records* for that set of tossing. So I reckon I got the last laugh in the end!

Being on television was great for my ego. But, brilliantly enough, it was also fantastic for my restaurants. In 1996, I had won my first major award – Best Italian Restaurant at the London Restaurant Awards – which had almost made me cry. Two years later, I really did cry at the Dorchester Hotel, when Zilli Fish was voted Best Media Restaurant in Carlton TV's Restaurant Awards.

I was on a roll. Signor Zilli was named Favourite Showbusiness Restaurant by Capital Radio listeners. I was on George Michael's table and Robbie Williams was one of the many big names to come back over to help celebrate the award with the team later that night. It was incredible stuff, because I had beaten places like The Ivy to get these awards, along with some of the oldest and best-known names in the capital.

It was an amazing feeling for someone who'd come to the country knowing no one and nothing all those years ago. And, while lots of food snobs might mock these awards and prefer to get Michelin stars, I couldn't have cared less. My restaurants have never been about formal, static, classical food served in a hushed atmosphere. I wanted mealtimes to be alive, the way they are in Italy. I didn't want to just feed people. I wanted to entertain them.

Anyway, winning Best Media and Favourite Showbusiness Restaurants was wonderful for me. Being part of the media and show-business worlds was just as good. I thrived on learning new skills and I never saw it as a problem if I was lousy at my first attempt. I've never been afraid to learn and I'm never too proud to ask for help.

Was I lucky that there were always so many industry insiders in my restaurants who I could ask for advice? Or had I created my own luck by building the kind of atmosphere in my restaurants that attracted the most interesting and creative of people? Either way, I was loving it. Business had hardly ever been better. My Zilli name had become a really powerful brand. Could it get much better?

My next challenge – or maybe my next joke – was to prove that cooking on television was only one of my many talents. I was going to start cooking on the radio as well. This kind of crazy idea could only have come from one man: Chris Evans. So listeners to his breakfast show would hear me crash and bash my pans around the studio to create my dish of the day. And we weren't faking anything – as listeners found out the morning I pulled out the wrong plug for my mini-cooker and forced Virgin Radio off air for nearly thirty terrible minutes!

The crisis apparently cost Virgin some £80,000 in lost advertising revenue. But they forgave me and Chris had me back the following week as if nothing had happened. That morning, we had a different problem. I'd forgotten the keys to the restaurant, so I hadn't been able to go and collect the ingredients or the equipment. Chris and I decided the show had to go on, and we did fake it that day. We clinked some cutlery together, we bashed around some plates from the station's canteen and we noisily pretended to chew our non-existent food. Amazingly, cooking on the radio was a hit. A few years later, I was doing it again on Classic FM with another good friend, Henry Kelly.

Anyway, the more Chris and I worked together, the closer we became. By now, I'd been on television so much that we were both getting recognised as we headed out on yet more benders. It probably encouraged us to be even wilder, though some nights that hardly seemed possible. To my shame, one evening we behaved so badly in a restaurant and made so much noise that a group of customers on nearby tables all refused to pay their bills.

The customers said, quite rightly, that the management should have thrown us out so everyone else could eat in peace. Unfortunately, I *was* the management – we were creating havoc in my own restaurant. It was a warning bell that my life was getting out of hand and I was risking some of the things I valued the most. I didn't hear it.

Away from Chris, my own life was still springing huge surprises – such as being asked to lunch at Buckingham Palace. It was a thank-you for a big fundraising event a lot of us West End restaurants had been part of. I'm not ashamed to say I was terrified. When the day came, I was also tearful. I kept thinking of my mother. She had worked so hard all her life. Her world had been so small, so tough. She had always been worrying, mainly about me. I desperately wanted her to know I was OK.

I couldn't imagine what she might have said if she had lived to see me have lunch at the Palace. I'd also spent so many years wanting my dad to notice me and recognise that I could make something of my life. Lunch at the Palace would pretty much have put an end to any arguments.

You get lots of information on how and where to arrive for these lunches, but I didn't find out where I was sitting until the very last moment. I was next to Prince Andrew. 'Zilli. How do you spell that?' he asked me, a mischievous look in his eye.

It turned out Andrew has a bit of a sense of humour as well. I'd been desperately worried that I would have nothing to say to him. But he was fun and very relaxed. So, after a while, I started to recount some of the stories about his brother Edward in my restaurant. It's not exactly protocol, but I suppose the royal family is a family like every other. Brothers love to find out what their siblings have been up to. Andrew certainly did.

Amazingly, once the formal meal was over, he offered me a mini-tour of the Palace. The only thing I can't remember about the occasion was the food. The chef in me should have been paying attention. The starstuck boy from an Italian village took over. As Andrew led me through what seemed like an endless series of Palace corridors, I was too excited to focus. When I left the Palace, it felt as if it had all been a dream. I hope my mum was looking down and saw me there. I hope she was proud of me.

Two other serious events were to break through the party scene of my life at this point. The first happened on Old Compton Street just around the corner from my restaurant. The second took place many thousands of miles south, in Cape Town. I hope my mother would have liked the way I reacted to both of them.

I was sitting outside Signor Zilli, chatting to Gary Kemp in the late-spring sunshine, when the Soho bomb went off. It exploded in the Admiral Duncan pub just a few hundred yards away on Old Compton Street. We could hear and feel it. Within minutes, when the first terrified people ran by, we found that it was serious. When we saw some people with blood on their clothes and faces, we knew we had to help.

We handed out water to anyone who looked like they needed it and we gave chairs to people who couldn't run any further. I felt a huge sense of anger that something so terrible had happened so close to me. Soho was my village; I wanted to defend it. Late that evening, we got a call from the police saying they thought there might be more bombs in the area. We had to evacuate the restaurant and wait for news elsewhere. My phone rang as my staff and I edged up Dean Street towards Soho Square.

It was Michelle Collins. She knew the quickest way to get from Signor Zilli to Zilli Fish was along Old Compton Street and that I did the walk half a dozen times a day. She just wanted to know I was safe. At home, I saw on the news that three people had been killed in the pub, including a woman who was four months pregnant. Her husband had been injured, the best man at their wedding and another friend of theirs had died. How could any man have done that?

Charity was the other big change that took me away from the party scene that year, and it sobered me up just as much as that awful bomb. It began when I was asked to go to South Africa to film a new series for Carlton Food Network. I couldn't agree fast enough. I practically ran to get on the plane. Cape Town is one of my favourite cities on earth. I loved the look and the feel of it. I loved the fish restaurants (The Codfather is a favourite, not least because it's one of the few places to have a sillier name than Zilli) and, of course, I loved all the local wines.

Ross Burden, Alan Coxon and I were there filming *Three Chefs in the Cape* – a sort of food, wine and travel show where we looked at all the local food and drink and showed how much fun you can have with it. It was a brilliant show to make. Who wouldn't want to be paid to fly to the sun and meet a load of brilliant new people?

But for me there was one unexpected part of the trip. It shook me up and wouldn't leave my mind. We filmed a few strands for the show in Red Cross Children's Hospital in Cape Town. Almost everything about that day stunned me. The awful condition of parts of the building, the standards of the beds, the equipment, the wards. And, most importantly, the simple goodness of the staff.

There was so much kindness in that hospital, so much good will. But, with no money, the patients just couldn't get all the help they deserved. I looked at the exhausted faces of the nurses, doctors and parents and felt something had to be done. Chris and I had one of our rare serious conversations. I felt I couldn't just walk away from those scenes. I'd come from nothing and now had so much. Those patients in Cape Town still had nothing. I had to help. Back in London, Chris and I came up with an idea for some fundraising with a difference. We would host a special evening at Zilli Fish and we would try to draw people in by persuading as many famous names as possible to cook in the kitchen, serve the food to the tables or, like Paul Young, man the karaoke machine.

It was a huge success. Thank you to everyone who answered my calls straight away and did me so proud on the night. It was a wild, chaotic night when so much could have gone wrong. But it was also the very best party of my year. The atmosphere was charged, because we were all doing it for a very specific reason.

We raised a lot of cash. I had arranged to ring the medical director of the hospital at midnight to tell him how much – if anything – we were able to send him. I was crying by the time I got through to him. The whole restaurant was waiting to hear the figure as well. But, because I'd seen the hospital first-hand, I knew more than anyone else just how much our money would mean. We had collected £50,000, and I vowed that we would try to beat the figure in a year's time. I had discovered a cause that mattered to me. After a few more years' fundraising, the hospital administrators said they wanted to name a ward after me. Can you ask for a better thing to achieve in life than that?

Sobering up because of bombs and hospitals made the first cracks appear in the Aldo and Chris show. We hit some bumps in the road just after the first charity evening, when we both flew down to Cape Town to physically hand over the cheque. The occasion meant so much to me. But Chris didn't seem to get it. He had met a new girl just before we left the UK, but that didn't seem to be a problem – Chris was always meeting new girls. We flew out overnight, checked into our hotel and then headed over to Camps Bay for lunch in the sun. It was a big lunch. We had four bottles of rosé, and then headed back to the hotel to sleep things off before the presentation the next day.

I slept like a baby and when my alarm went off at 8pm I jumped out of bed. I was buzzing with instant excitement about what we were going to do. I rang Chris's room to check his alarm had gone off, but didn't get a reply. I thought I knew where he would be, though, and headed down to the bar. No sign of him. He wasn't sleeping it off by the pool either. He wasn't anywhere else in sight. I headed to the front desk.

'Oh, Mr Evans has checked out.'

'I'm sorry, what?'

'He checked out a couple of hours ago.'

'But we only arrived this morning.'

'Well, he's no longer in the hotel, Mr Zilli.'

Chris and I were both expected at the presentation ceremony at the hospital the following day. But I was there on my own. As I handed over the cheque, Chris was climbing off his plane back in Britain, chasing the girl he had met just before leaving – someone I doubt he can even remember today.

We hardly spoke for a month after I got back to the UK. Then Chris came round to Signor Zilli and practically broke down my office door so he could apologise in person. We soon fell back into our old routine. Back then, we had so many rows, so many ups and downs. It was exactly like being married, but without the sex. So what did we decide to do next? Bearing in mind all the tension, we had our stupidest idea yet. We decided to go into business together.

CHAPTER EIGHTEEN

Big Business

Like most things with Chris, it all began as joke. 'Why don't we start our own company? We could call it Zilli Chris,' he said one day.

I laughed at the idea. But Chris had caught me at a weak moment. I was itching to expand and I knew exactly where I wanted to go.

Over the past few years, I had got to know Notting Hill. It was a fantastic part of London. I loved the markets and food stores and thought it had the same village feel I had recognised in Soho all those years ago. I felt I'd be happy as a new lord of the manor there. I was convinced that a Zilli restaurant was just what the area needed.

But I was also getting carried away by the ongoing march towards super-size restaurants. Quaglino's, Mezzo and all the others had defied the critics and were still pulling in the punters. I didn't want to be left behind and the theatre crowds who filled out Signor Zilli and

Zilli Fish told me I had to open in Covent Garden as well. With Chris in my corner, I reckoned I could do both. So I got to work; I got serious about Zilli Chris.

Straight away, I found two fantastic sites – one in Notting Hill, the other in Covent Garden. I had plans drawn up. I started to really see the dream – then I saw Chris lose interest. It could have been that his accountants were against the idea. It could have been that he didn't want to mix business with pleasure. It could have been anything. But I'd passed the point of no return by the time Zilli Chris got canned. I was on my own, the way I'd always been, so I vowed to carry on the way I always had.

My site in Notting Hill cost £120,000 and I spent £80,000 kitting out what the previously enthusiastic Chris had suggested we call 'Zilli?'. The question mark came because neither of us could think of the next word! We wrote it down on a napkin as a question and reckoned it worked. 'Just leave it like that,' Chris said. 'It'll get noticed.' But it didn't really do the trick the right way. It was silly, not Zilli – though I didn't spot this for quite some time.

Almost all the money for the expansion came from Zilli Fish. It was booming and it turned out that I couldn't have timed my move west any better. Hugh Grant and Julia Roberts were about to make Notting Hill world famous with a film. One lunchtime, Hugh came in and asked for a 'hangover cure' for lunch. We decided a really thick spaghetti Bolognese would do the trick. It turned him into a regular, so we must have been right. Gwyneth Paltrow had dinner just after we had opened and the rest of the Notting Hill set were desperate for new places to spend daddy's money. I was so hot back then I was on fire.

Over in Covent Garden, things were really heating up as well. The site I wanted over there was an old bank building that would need to be gutted from top to bottom. I needed £1 million for the work, but before I even started I had something else to spend my money on.

The tiny corner site next to Zilli Fish on Brewer Street had come up for sale. It was the last part of the block that I had always wanted, and it was now or never to buy it. So £480,000 disappeared on acquiring it and having a total café interior built in Venice and shipped over to Soho. In Covent Garden, meanwhile, I was getting a crash course on how much had changed since I'd tarted up Signor Zilli with a lick of paint, some new tablecloths and reopened after just a weekend's work. Health & Safety no longer let amateurs loose on anything open to the public. Its long list of requirements began with lifts for disabled customers and never seemed to end. Things I'd never thought about or heard of were essential if I was to be allowed to trade. And the money kept pouring out.

I'm not someone who lives easily with debt – I'd rather cut my losses and move on. I struggled with the idea that I would have to spend so much for so long before getting any return. If I wasn't having sleepless nights after boozing with Chris and our friends, I'd be having them because I was suddenly worried about all the money I was spending.

I tried to focus on the good stuff. My favourite bit of

Covent Garden was to be a wood-burning pizza oven, something I had wanted ever since my childhood in Italy. I still think you can taste how and where food has actually been cooked. I wanted to lift my pizzas out of the ordinary and give a true taste of Italy. I just had to try to put the cost out of my mind. My designer, Sam, was back on board doing the interiors at Covent Garden; our 'squid' light fittings made me smile, even though the 200 seats we would have to fill each day practically made me cry.

I knew we had to make bold statements to succeed in theatreland. The pared-down look of Zilli Fish wouldn't have worked. We needed something grand, something lavish and opulent. We got it – once we'd paid for it. Sam had created splashes of blue and other rich colours to keep the interior alive. There were big flashy mirrors on the stairs, lots of life everywhere. All we needed were bums on seats and after such a long rebuild I was itching to open.

It was snowing in March 2001 when Zilli Fish Too finally opened. There was a big England game on, so we had a lot of competition as the hottest ticket in town. The press and the paparazzi were out in force and it was standing room only all night. Zilli Fish Too seemed to be what everyone wanted. I was there every day for a couple of months because I was so obsessed with my new toy – the wood-burning oven.

Because we had so much space in Covent Garden, I had brought back the idea of having kids' Sundays. We would have face-painting and pizza-making downstairs for the kids, while parents could relax on the ground floor. Michelle Collins, Patsy Palmer and their families were all big supporters of the idea. Their loud laughter and enthusiasm made the place so much more fun to run. And Michelle's party for her daughter Maia was one of the best we had there.

But I have to admit that having four restaurants, plus the Signor Zilli Bar and new Zilli Café, was pretty exhausting. It was just as well I had a new surge of energy back then. If I can't be superman I can at least be superchef, I decided. I had gone back to my Italian roots and got myself a scooter to try to beat London traffic and zip from one restaurant to another.

I would cook and go, cook and go all day. Trouble was, I was sticking to my Italian roots in the way I watched the road as well. I would forget about it all together if any pretty girls were near by. After a few near misses, I hit real trouble one day when I was trying to get to Notting Hill from Soho. I was taking a load of fresh pasta with me when I – and the pasta – went flying. I landed on the road, the pasta landed on a Mercedes – a convertible Mercedes with the top down. I still feel bad about ruining that man's day. And his leather interior.

That summer, I needed my scooter for other reasons as well. One morning our whole food delivery was stolen from the street outside Zilli Fish. I had to join the rest of the staff on an emergency Tesco run to replace the missing bits before the customers arrived. Even this seemed good fun at the time, and we all had a laugh trying to make sure it was business as usual later in the day.

Zilli Fish Too had started getting some great reviews, even from the snootiest restaurant critics. One of them actually said in his piece that he had turned up determined to hate the place, but that the atmosphere and the food had won him around. So some days I managed to stop worrying about money for as much as a couple of hours at a time. I managed to forget that nearly ninety people relied on me for their wages or that my bank debts were still sky high.

Looking back, it's just as well I built up the Zilli brand without Chris. I think if we had set up a company together we might have ended up killing each other. Mixing business with pleasure isn't a good idea. And Chris and I were still having fun. In those good times, we still liked to play silly games. One of them was to set ourselves ridiculous challenges. The best one Chris set himself got him in the papers every day for months. 'By the end of the day, I'm going to be going out with a Spice Girl,' he vowed one lazy morning when we were at a loose end.

He did it. Top target was Baby Spice, Emma Bunton, but he couldn't get through to her and the clock was ticking. What he needed was a Spice Girl with something to promote. Enter, stage left, Geri Halliwell, whose solo career was never out of the papers. I had seen one of the top *Daily Mirror* journalists in the restaurant that day and I would have loved to give him the story. I'd even written a headline to go with it: GINGER AND SPICE. But I kept quiet. I wanted to see how this would end.

By the end of the day, Chris had won his challenge. He was dating Geri, though he soon ended up with a lot more than he had bargained for. Geri had been due to appear on *TFI Friday* that week, which had made the initial contact a lot easier. Going on a date with Chris meant he could collect on his bet and she could get on to the front pages.

But I don't think Chris expected what happened next.

Geri came round to his house for dinner and practically moved in – she had her belongings with her. They might have been in this for a laugh and for some publicity, but it soon had Chris running for the exits. Chris moves on fast when he has had enough of someone. Only Billie Piper would be different – at least for a while.

I met little Billie at the Met Bar, at the time one of the coolest places in London and a surprising place for someone so young. She was bright and sparky and hid her tiredness pretty well. Next day Chris was having a business lunch at Zilli Fish as usual and I told him.

'Billie Piper? You met Billie Piper?'

'Yes. She's cool. Have you met her?'

'Yes and I want to meet her again. She was on *TFI* and I loved her. Have you got her number?'

'No, we only talked for a while. She's about twenty years too young for me.'

'Tosser. You should have got her number.'

And so began another giant ginger sulk. But Chris soon swung into action. On the Friday of that week, I was on my way to Virgin Radio's studios over in Golden Square to do my usual cooking slot. Also on the show was the still sparky Billie Piper. I'd seen Chris with so many women by now, but that morning he was very clearly a different man. He had seen something in Billie that matched him. He needed her to know it too.

The Chris Evans Breakfast Show was the jewel in

Virgin's crown. Hour after hour of great music, ridiculous fun and madness – and my wonderful cooking slot. But the banter when Billie was in the studio was wilder than ever. Only the production team and I could see it, but the pair really did swap shirts on air. And Chris really did look just a little too closely at Billie's body in the process. Meanwhile, I looked at our producer and the rest of the team. Something different was going on here. None of us could get a word in edgeways that morning after all.

At the end of the show, it made more great radio when Chris asked Billie to marry him and she said yes. But, while I didn't for a second think it would ever happen, I could tell they would at least start some kind of relationship. I didn't know I'd have so many ringside seats to it, though.

The first proof of how serious Chris had become came later that week, when he was having a small Christmas lunch for some of his colleagues at Signor Zilli. He started off with a few beers in Zilli Bar and then disappeared. I tracked him down in one of our usual pubs near by and he said he needed to take a call from Billie before coming back to the lunch. But he never showed up, so I served the Christmas meal without him. Back at the restaurant, we all said it must be love. And it looked as if it might be.

A couple of days later, we found out he had bought Billie the infamous £105,000 Ferrari.

Chris called me from the HR Owen showroom in Knightsbridge. 'I'm just about to do something,' he said. It was clearly something big. You could always tell with Chris.

'What is it?'

'I'm buying her a car,' he said. Then he told me exactly what car. I nearly dropped the phone.

'All you bought me was a bleeding golf club!' I told him.

'Aldo, mate, I'm not planning to get inside your knickers.'

Can't argue with that.

Anyway, our conversation wasn't quite over. 'Ring the press, will you?' he asked me, telling me exactly where they would be able to get a good shot of the car. When I checked he wasn't joking I called the *Sun*. So was this just another wild publicity stunt? At first, I thought it was. But over time I could tell how serious Chris was about Billie. The pair were in the middle of a storm.

The press went wild over every detail of Chris and Billie's relationship. She was the golden girl of pop whom the tabloids reckoned was already going off the rails. He was the bad influence, twice her age, who might be the one to push her. But there was nothing false about the fun they had. They connected, right from the off. So what if he was older? Most of the time he acted like a five-year-old. She was far more grown-up than he was. They met in the middle and it worked.

We all had some great benders in the early days of that relationship. Billie had stamina and she was up for anything. And, by taking over as Chris's drinking companion in chief, she gave my liver a well-earned break – though it was only a temporary one.

Chris and Billie had got married in Las Vegas and were off drinking bars dry around the world. When they came back to London, we had a real blow-out of a drinking session to celebrate. And I got a real wake-up call about my future. It was June and Chris and I ended up in all our old haunts – we started in the Blue Post in Soho, headed over to the Nag's Head in Knightsbridge and ended up in Stringfellows. But I think we went to about a million other bars in between.

As part of the session, I remember that someone was sick in the street and someone had a pee in the middle of the pavement. At least one of those people might have been me.

That three-day bender ended with Chris saying goodbye to Virgin Radio, though that whole period is pretty much a blur. When Chris and Billie then headed off to party some more in Portugal and Los Angeles, I had to face up to reality about my own marriage. It was over. It just needed to be made official.

Divorce wasn't even in my language as a child – it wasn't a word I ever heard. My parents had married for life and, however hard their relationship had been, they would never have separated. They ultimately died so soon after each other that they never really lived apart. They were my role model: totally flawed, but they stayed together.

In 21st-century Great Britain, Jan and I could never do that. But while life had changed, divorce was still a word I didn't want to hear. Having gone through the process, it's not something I would wish on my worst enemy. The only good thing about my divorce was that I managed to keep it private and mostly out of the papers. However, I'm not sure it could have come at a worse time. The financial side of things had taken ages for the experts to settle and all the values seemed to have been added up in the good times. They would have to be paid in the bad.

Business had been suffering badly ever since the terrible events of 11 September 2001. Like everyone else I stared at the television screens in shock when the planes hit the Twin Towers. The news had broken towards the end of our lunchtime service and we knew about it because far more mobile phones started to ring than normal.

A lot of shocked faces passed the news on to their fellow diners and the restaurant emptied fast. The financial effects would be with us for a long time – far longer than the first Gulf War. I was back worrying about money twenty-four hours a day. I couldn't see how I could pay my divorce settlement; I worried about the future of my staff and about my own. I felt sick so much of the day, right to my stomach. And that's not good when you're a chef.

I tried desperately to think of other things, to find new challenges and to get my optimism and my sunshine back. One idea that succeeded was to write another cookbook – that always cheered me up. I'd done the first one back in 1998, *Aldo's Italian Food For Friends*, and I always tried to keep it simple. I learned my cooking from instinct rather than firm rules. I want people to know it's worth giving things a try.

We always give the first drafts out to the other halves of our staff – the people who don't have anything to do with restaurants. If they enjoy and say it works, then it's in. If they get confused or struggle with anything, we sort it out. The last thing I want to do is make anyone's life harder. And it does seem to work. I love it when people come up and tell me they used one of my recipes for a big dinner party or a special meal. I sign a lot of copies in my restaurants and I enjoy it.

In 2001, my latest book was *Aldo Zilli's Foolproof Italian Cookery* and I headed back for a break in my old home town to do some research and put it all together. Coming back from Italy that autumn, I could tell immediately that things were still tough after 9/11. I could feel a real sense of nervousness in London. A fear of spending money, of having too good a time. London was having a strangely warm autumn that year, but I felt cold all the time. I was feeling sick again, always worried, hardly sleeping. I started making mistakes.

Up west in Notting Hill, I was starting to have real problems. For the whole of the following year, the restaurant there was even colder than I was. My focus had been on Covent Garden for so long that I would go weeks without visiting Kensington Park Road up in W11. But if *I* couldn't be bothered to go to that restaurant, then why should anyone else? There's nothing like a hot restaurant to create a buzz. But when the climate changes, it can change for good. I couldn't stop worrying about it, but I didn't know how to turn things around.

When I did visit the restaurant at the height of the crisis, I couldn't believe what I saw. What the hell has happened to the fish?'

'They're dying,' my very perceptive restaurant manager informed me.

'Well, of course they're dying. Look at the state of the water. What are you feeding them?'

'Sardines.'

I swung round to look at my manager, a man from my own region out in Italy. 'Sardines? To tropical fish? What are you thinking of?'

Of course, he hadn't been thinking anything at all. He had just lobbed the fish the first thing that came to hand. And why not? It must have felt to him as if he was being ignored on the edge of an empire that had long since moved east. True, years previously I'd killed a load of lobsters in my Zilli Fish tank, so maybe I couldn't complain too much. But it all told me how out of control things had become.

As it turned out I couldn't stop that long in Notting Hill. As if I wasn't busy enough, I was suddenly going to be on TV all the time. My agents were fielding loads of calls about different shows and I was keen to do as many as possible. Filming *Dinner Dates* for ITV was the first part of the strategy – and I was on a steep learning curve. By now, I was totally relaxed cooking on camera and doing my own thing. But sticking to a script took a bit of concentration and I got really nervous waiting for all the cameras to be set up. Still, that was nothing to my next job. I'd agreed to face Anne Robinson on *The Weakest Link*.

It was a 'chefs' special' and I was up there with the likes of Antony Worrall Thompson, Sophie Grigson and Nick Nairn. We all acted tough, though I thought I was going to pee in my pants. The good news is, we didn't really have to spend much time with Anne. She even had a 'body double' stand in to set up the publicity photographs. She is scary when she arrives, though. On set you don't get a break from her tough-cookie act.

She took the mickey out of my clothes. (Doesn't everyone?) And I didn't even win. In fact, I was the second to come off, I think, and I lost on a food question. It was mortifying. Funnily enough, since then I've met Anne several times socially and she's a completely different woman out of the studio. Relaxed, warm and funny. I just wish I'd known that before I went on her show. Anyway, it was all good stuff to get the Zilli name out there.

Things were still tough in the restaurant business, though. By 2003, every restaurant owner in the country seemed to be feeling the pinch. How long would this slump last? I still loved Notting Hill, and I was so afraid of looking like a failure, but, in the end, I knew I had to let that restaurant go. It was making money, just not enough of it. I put up the For Sale sign, hoping that the money raised would protect the rest of my business. But, with so much other money going out back then, it wasn't enough. I was back juggling money every day, worrying about it every hour. How simple life had been in the past; how frighteningly responsible it was now.

In Covent Garden, Zilli Fish Too needed to bring in £50,000 or £60,000 a week, every week. It had to be full to survive. The rent, the rates, the staff, the debts.

'Is it all my fault? Have I pissed it all away?' I woke to those questions every morning, tried to sleep with them ringing in my mind every night. In my worst moments that summer, I tried to add up how much I had been drinking and how much I had been losing. It's so easy to take your eye off the ball in life and in any type of business. It's harder to recover ground once you've lost it.

I should have seen that only the champagne companies and the breweries were benefiting from these crazy years with Chris and all the others. What I needed to know now was how fast I could grow up and deal with the fall-out. Suppliers were constantly on our case over their bills, but I was no longer in a world where I always had plenty of cash coming in and could pay everyone straight away. I could always get the money, but I had to wait for Peter before I could pay Paul. Not surprisingly, Paul didn't like it. And there were a lot more Pauls than Peters.

Some days, I would be physically sick with worry over the money pouring out of my business. I had endless stomach pains which, it turned out, were being caused by an ulcer. I felt exhausted, run down and lost. I felt as if I had aged twenty years. When I looked in the mirror I thought it must be true. All the time I felt I was being chased by failure and by ghosts. I could picture my dad, doing all his sums in his head, watching everything on the way in and everything on the way out. He had never missed a single stolen watermelon! He would be horrified at how much I had let slip. And, as the months went by, it got worse and worse.

'Oh God. No. Not this.' I froze when I read the newspaper article. One of my suppliers had gone to the press. We had been waiting for a payment to come in to us before we paid them, but they wanted their money now. Basically, the story suggested that I couldn't pay my bills. It was a cleverly written article, full of rumours and theories. I couldn't sue, because it didn't say anything specific. But you couldn't miss the message. It pretty much said I might lose everything. It made it look as if I was going bust. And it was Christmas.

We had already decided that Zilli Fish Too would close for a refurbishment once the Christmas party season ended. When I recovered fully from my ulcer, I wanted a big loud push for a New Year reopening. But my accountants said no. 'You can't save it,' they told me. 'It's past the point where it can get better. If you don't act now, you could lose everything.'

So my wonderful Zilli Fish Too never reopened. All the good times there were forgotten. Many of my staff had to find other jobs. No one had a happy new year.

We did a voluntary liquidation, or something like that. It was complicated, ugly and depressing. The restaurant was sold and the money raised paid back the banks. So much of the rest of the money we had spent in Covent Garden had been mine; it never came back. The £150,000 rent deposit I had paid? Not returned. It was terrible. And I had to face up to my part of it. A ship won't sink if the captain is good at his job. You can't lose a war and blame your soldiers.

In just a handful of wild years, I reckoned I had lost £2 million. I had lost two restaurants. And if I didn't quit the booze and sort out my lifestyle I could lose my health as well. I knew I was carrying too much weight and living too badly. And I was supposed to be the king of light, healthy eating. How had I forgotten that?

It wasn't exactly easy to relax, though. One more financial storm would break before I turned the corner. This one came out of nowhere. After the sale of my Notting Hill site, I got new accountants. To this day I'm not sure what happened, but all I know is that after seeing plenty of money going into the bank I'd ended up with a lot less than I had expected once the outstanding bills were paid.

Even then, my new accountants said Signor Zilli, Zilli Fish, the bar and the café could still be at risk. It was devastating. These places were where the real memories were buried. Dean Street was where I had begun. How could I save it all?

I kicked myself for letting things like this slip. Whenever I think I don't have what it takes to deal with financial affairs, I think about how my dad ran his business despite being unable to read or write. If he could use his brain to account for every lira and centesimo then I could watch the pounds and pennies in the UK.

Today, I can't really say how the figures worked out because everything was so complicated. All I knew was that I would do anything it took to get through this storm. I had to prove myself both financially and physically, because there was something very new in my life. In 2004, after so long searching, I had already met someone amazing. She was tall, beautiful and endlessly intriguing. I was in love. Her name was Nikki.

CHAPTER NINETEEN

Nikki

A strong wind was blowing and a stunning, willowy young woman was crossing the road outside Zilli Fish Too. That was always a good thing. And as I parked my car outside it looked as if she was about to join a friend inside for a drink. Even better. I left the car and headed in to play host. Something told me I had to meet this girl.

'Hi, I'm Aldo.'

'I'm Nikki. Nice to meet you.'

And that was it. Just an ordinary meeting on an ordinary day. But I knew, somehow, that I didn't want it to stop there. I was hardly surprised to find out that Nikki was working as a model – she was the best-looking woman we had seen at our bar in ages, and we got a lot of beautiful women at Zilli Fish Too. Nikki had just been modelling for Versace, across the street, so I told my story about Gianni's party, years ago. She laughed. I liked that.

Nikki had a fantastic figure and the deepest, most beautiful eyes I'd ever seen. Plus, she had a naughty smile. She had spirit. She looked brave. I couldn't take my eyes off her. Problem was, I had to. I'd come over to Covent Garden for a business meeting. Gianni, one of my close friends, was hosting a dinner with one of my sponsors. I had a horrible feeling I was going to have to face a couple of hours sitting with a group of men in suits. Just what I didn't want.

'Aldo, I think they're ready for you.' One of my staff tapped me on the shoulder.

Somehow, I hadn't noticed how long we had been at the bar or that so many diners had arrived, including my own dinner guests. 'You know what, I really don't fancy this,' I said.

Nikki smiled cheekily. It turned out that she really was naughty. 'I'll come with you, if you like,' she said. 'But only if I can sit next to you.'

It would be like the restaurant scene in *Pretty Woman*, though hopefully without the snail shells flying across the room.

'This is my assistant, Nikki,' I said, very aware of how closely Gianni and the other men looked at this tall, beautiful woman. None of them was brave enough to point out that I had never had an assistant called Nikki before. Or that my real assistant, the wonderful Louisa Alves, was already at the table. But Nikki and I were enjoying the joke. It was the first of so many I wanted us to share.

The meal and the meeting lasted two hours – the longest two hours in my life, but not the worst, because every bit of me was aware of how close Nikki was sitting. When coffee arrived, she put her hand on my knee. We had to leave. Fast.

'This way, there's a back door.'

We rushed our goodbyes and bundled past the Staff Only signs. We headed to my car. We were laughing like kids. I felt like I was running away from school.

'So, how old are you?'

Nikki was twenty-five.

'Well, how old are you?'

I couldn't tell her. All my life I have felt the wrong age. When I was young, I had to act old. When I was looking for work, I had to lie about my age. When I rented Il Siciliano in Soho, no one could believe my age. When I was partying with Chris Evans, I certainly didn't act my age. Till now, none of this had ever mattered. So many of my friends had been older than me. Nino, all my favourite chefs, my first girlfriend and my first wife had all been older than me. Did it matter that Nikki was so much younger? I admitted I was forty-six and I got my answer:

'Age is just a number,' Nikki said. It didn't mean a thing to her.

We went away on holiday together within two weeks of meeting. A week in Sardinia, where we could really find each other. We stayed in the most romantic hotel, far from anywhere. It was a week of good food and great love. And we did find each other, in the middle of our ages. She was so much older, I was so much younger. This was going to work. My face ached from smiling. My brain ached from counting my lucky stars. But was this just a holiday romance?

I worried so much. Maybe it was the wine, the sunshine and the long, lovely days that were blinding us to reality. Would this wonderful lady up and leave me when we got back to London? Every day I tried to second-guess what she might be thinking. But I soon realised I didn't need to. What you see really is what you get with Nikki. She was so fresh, so honest, so fun. It felt so good to be with someone who wasn't hiding anything.

The face ache from smiling came back.

In London, we started living together pretty much straight away. Yes, it was fast, but if you know something is right then you know it. Why not go for it? Nikki's aunt was Italian and she had been there almost every summer when she was growing up. (That's how she got to surprise me in Sardinia by speaking Italian to some of our hotel staff.) So it turned out we met in the middle on our nationalities as well. Sometimes I think I've become much more English than her. She can be more Italian than me. Nikki and I match.

'You should meet my family.'

We were planning another trip back to Italy and I wanted to show how serious I was about her. Like I say, Nikki knew Italy. She knew what big Italian families were like. She knew this wasn't going to be an easy ride, but she agreed to it without a second thought. When the Zillis get together, we seem to go on forever. Brothers, sisters-in-law, cousins, children and children's children.

Marisa and my brother Giacomino still live in my parents' old house in Alba Adriatica, though it's finally got proper electricity and running water. It's a happy house at last. Nikki did me so proud when we got there. She charmed them all, even Pasquale the priest, who is the hardest sell of the bunch. He had been the most suspicious of this young pretty girl on his little brother's arm. Before he met her, Pasquale was thinking that, having failed in his marriage, his crazy little brother had clearly lost his mind. Now he and Nikki are thick as thieves.

Thankfully, it's the same with Nikki and my daughter Laura. I was convinced that they would get along if they met as friends. But would the fact that Nikki was my new partner get in the way of that? Laura had taken the divorce hard all those years ago and I didn't want to jeopardise the great friendship we now had. Fortunately, it never came to that. She and Nikki met at a birthday dinner I held for Laura at the Sanderson Hotel. They got on like a house on fire – not least because they are practically the same size and could share clothes. I remember one of the proudest moments of my life was seeing Laura on a catwalk before winning a modelling competition in a shopping centre. Now I had two beautiful models in my life. And they're good friends. That was about as good as things could get.

In London, I know some of my friends were worrying as well. I pretty much disappeared off the scene. I saw no one, because the only person I wanted to see was Nikki. The gap between everyone's fears and the truth makes me laugh. Friends thought I was being led astray by this tall young model. Maybe I was at wild parties, they thought, drinking, doing drugs, falling apart.

Instead, we were at home. It took me too many years

to realise that domestic bliss really can exist. I also learned that bad times aren't something to run from. Surviving them should make relationships stronger. And Nikki and I were to be tested right from the start.

The first issue was my business. Nikki was one of the few to know just how much debt I was in and how hard I would have to work to rebuild my business. She saw me face the figures and have panic attacks over paying my bills. She knew how afraid I was and she put up with this for years. Thankfully for us, her own career was on a roll and she had already earned a lot of money. She owned her own apartment and had bought another one to rent out as an investment. She was focused and ambitious and clever with money. Everyone likes to joke that models are airheads. Not this one. No one else knew it, but it was Nikki's cash that saw us through the worst times.

She also invested a lot of time in our relationship – teaching me what I should have known already. She turned down some of the big modelling jobs that came her way if they meant too much travelling and time apart, but she took on so many more. She kept the roof over our heads when I thought I might lose that as well. It's because of Nikki that I was able to rebuild the Zilli name into what it is today.

As we did so, though, we had another terrible challenge to face. Nikki's wonderful dad Brian had been diagnosed with cancer. She had always been incredibly close to him. As a black-cab driver, he had taken her to all her early modelling jobs, waiting outside for hours and supporting her as she made her dreams come true. Now it was our turn to try to support him.

Just before Brian died, we held a small family dinner party at Zilli Fish for his birthday. It was a quiet, lovely evening. And, at the end of it, something magical happened. As we were preparing to leave, Brian made a point of saying that Nikki should go home with me. It was as if he was giving his daughter away, giving his total consent to our relationship. The date, Brian's birthday, was 4 March. It was to have incredible significance to us both from then on.

Brian dealt with his cancer with real dignity and proved to be a true gentleman. His death came fast, though, and Nikki took it so hard. She was strong and brave enough to sing at his funeral, but in private I saw my strong, beautiful and open woman close up to the world as she grieved. She became introverted, difficult, increasingly tough on herself and everything around her. The blackness lasted for almost a year; her love for her dad had been so strong.

I bought us a puppy one day to try to make Nikki smile again. She was a tiny Shar Pei who turned out to be as feisty as her new owner. She was a little dog with a big mission: she wanted to wreck our house! After less than three months, we decided it wasn't working out and the little monster headed off to some different owners. Nikki, though, had indeed started smiling again, so the puppy had done what I'd hoped for and a few ruined carpets didn't matter at all.

Nikki, of course, showed how it should really have been done when she bought our next pets as a Valentine's Day present: two goldfish called Romeo and Juliet. High on romance, low on maintenance. I should have thought of that myself.

Aldo the showman still did his thing in the restaurants through all these private problems. I carried on looking at our menus, darted in and out of all the kitchens and tried to make every guest feel welcome by walking around as many tables as possible.

Talking to strangers always lifted me out of my troubles. And what's the point of cooking great food if you can't see people enjoy it? I loved finding out that the quiet, comfortable couple in the corner were having a wedding anniversary. That the girl in the middle of the big table of office workers was heading off to start a new life in America. Or that the tourists had read about the 'mad Italian Aldo Zilli' in their home country and were checking him out on their holiday. All human life really does eat out in London. No two days will ever be the same if you take the time to talk to your customers.

A phone call from my agent was about to turn my life around again, though at the time it didn't sound like the nicest of calls.

'How fat are you?' Fiona asked me.

'Mind your own business,' I replied.

But then she explained. She told me about the bizarre-sounding show called *Celebrity Fit Club*. For a while, I still thought it was a wind-up, but she persisted. 'The money is good and it will be great exposure,' she said.

But there was a catch. If I wasn't fat enough, I couldn't take part.

'Go and weigh yourself,' Fiona told me.

So I did and got great news: I was officially obese. I could sign up for the show.

Nikki and I were lounging around at home later that night. 'So, how exactly is it going to work?'

I was trying to remember everything that the producer had told me. 'They get a group of us together, put us on some kind of exercise regime and try and make us fit. It's a health show.'

'So you live in, like *Big Brother*?'

I was stopped in my tracks. 'Bloody hell, I hope not. I don't think that was what he said.'

'Well, how will they measure who gets fit?'

'They have doctors and sports people who test us at the start and throughout the show. It's done over weeks and weeks.'

'So you'd better not be living in.'

I held her hand. 'No way. But I probably could do with getting fit again.'

The cocky, vain, peacock from Italy had got lost after so many years of hard city living. The long hair? Long gone. The tanned Italian skin? Lost to grey old London. And the fit body? 'I look like shit.' I stood up in front of Nikki, this stunning young model who now shared my life.

'I like how you look.'

'But I should look better. I could do.'

'Then do the show. Get fit. I'll help if you want.'

I sat thinking for the rest of the evening. If I wanted to get fit, I could do it with Nikki's help. I could join a gym again, get a trainer; Nikki and I could go on runs together. But would I follow through? Did I need the pressure of a television show to keep going? I needed her advice again. 'It could be humiliating,' I told her.

'Are they voting people off? Is it like *I'm A Celebrity*?'

'No. It's supposed to be serious. It's like an experiment. They want to show that people really can change their lives if they get the right advice.'

'So it just happens to be celebrities on the show?'

'Exactly. But I don't know if I want to show my belly.'

We both looked at it. Nikki started to laugh.

'Maybe that's what you need to do. Show the nation what a pig you've turned into. Then you'll have to do something about it.'

I looked at her. I wasn't sure I really wanted this kind of tough love. But I knew she was right. I needed to kick-start my life and a public wake-up call would probably be the loudest I could find. This also felt like the right time for me. I loved Nikki. I didn't want to miss out on any part of our new life together. I didn't want to die early, just another fat middle-aged man who forgot that heart attacks could kill. I called the producers the next day. I signed up to *Celebrity Fit Club*. Best decision I had made in years.

My first weigh-in was traumatic. I knew what the scales would say, but I didn't want to hear it. And I didn't want the world to know the truth. The body measurements were just as humiliating. That wasn't a waist measurement – it was a phone number. How had I let myself fall apart like this? Where had that wiry Italian lad gone? My fellow celebrities were the ultimate mixed bunch – just as the producers had intended. Julie Goodyear was clearly determined to be the Queen Bee, reliving her Bet Lynch days from *Coronation Street*. Paul Ross was there desperately trying to be Jonathan Ross.

Lizzie Bardsley from *Wife Swap* was there to shock me every time she opened her mouth.

Right from day one I felt differently about the programme to most of the others, because I had decided to do this for real. It wasn't a television show to me, it was medical. I wanted to give myself a future. I was forty-seven years old. Every forty-something man who has let things slip should do the same. After the group of us had all been probed, prodded and recorded for the start of the show, the hard work began. The producers hadn't stinted on finding the right experts. Getting really professional advice on diet, exercise and the way the body works was invaluable and I would carry on quizzing the instructors long after the cameras had gone away. Fortunately, Harvey Walden IV was nowhere near as scary as his name. Each week we would be weighed and checked out to see if the regime was working.

As time passed, I gravitated towards Tina Baker, who seemed to be as serious as I was about the challenge. I genuinely didn't want to play up to the cameras like some, though of course the whole point of reality television is that we all forget ourselves and act like idiots at some point. And with me, that point is never too far away. So I know I was a bit of a plonker a lot of the time. ('Plonker' – that's another of my favourite British words!)

Anyway, however embarrassing it was to almost bare all on the show, I never regretted being part of it. I learned a lot. I lost all the weight I wanted to – nearly three stone in total – and I got a strategy to keep it off. And I somehow got a huge burst of new energy. Fit people can do more. If you're fat and full of junk food, you're more likely to be depressed; you don't like how you look, of course, so you get even more depressed. And it all gets worse. No wonder you won't want to get out of bed in the morning and start to hate life.

Get fit at forty, fifty, any age, and you change all of that. Sex gets better, too. But, while you want to be in bed for that, I found I wanted to get out of bed in the mornings again and get going with my day. Just as well, because that was exactly when I was working so hard to get my restaurants through their crisis.

'Aldo, you look fantastic.'

'Aldo! I hardly recognise you. You look amazing.'

'Aldo, it's taken years off you.'

Yes, it's boastful to repeat all that. But I really did start to get compliments when the *Fit Club* routine kicked it. People noticed – though I admit that's less because I looked like a Greek god afterwards and more because I looked like a porky little Italian beforehand! Praise is always nice, though, so bring it on. Diet has always been important to me, but after *Fit Club* I focused on it even more. Even better, I knew my restaurants could benefit from it.

CHAPTER TWENTY

New Friends

Halfway through *Fit Club*, Nikki and I booked a holiday in Barbados to celebrate my new lifestyle. I felt more confident about being on a beach than I had in years, but I had another reason for looking forward to the trip.

'I've got a booking at your hotel later this month. I wanted to find something out. Can you help arrange weddings on the beach?' I was on the phone from my Brewer Street office. I hadn't got a plan at this stage, just an idea. I wanted to know if it might come together.

'That's great news, thank you. I just wanted to find out. We'll see you soon.' I hung up. I already knew that Nikki wouldn't want a huge, old-fashioned wedding. She still missed her dad so much. I wanted her wedding day to be filled with sunshine and laughter. And with no father-of-the-bride to give her away, I knew a traditional day would always carry a heavy shadow of sadness.

'You know we're going to get married, don't you?'

As wedding proposals go, it was hardly the most romantic of phrases. Who says Italians are smooth with this kind of thing? Nikki and I were packing for our trip to The House, a fantastic thirty-room boutique hotel on the island. She sat as still as a statue.

'What did you say?'

'That we're going to get married. I know we are.'

'OK.' Hardly the most romantic of acceptances, so we're even.

'They could do it in Barbados.'

'I don't want anyone there. I want it to be just us.'

'So do I.'

And that was it. We flew out for our two-week trip and my old friend Gianni and I got the ball rolling the day we arrived. The hotel and its staff were wonderful. They understood how romantic we wanted it, but how simple it had to be. It was our day. Ours alone. Some of the hotel staff were our witnesses and we said our vows barefoot in the famous white sand. I had flown in an old friend, Rob Gross, to take the photographs and he did us proud, capturing each mood of that special day. Finally, we released two white doves and had our first kiss as husband and wife. It was spiritual, energising and lovely.

It was also a great laugh. Even before the ceremony we had been in stitches over Nikki's make-up. The beauty staff in the hotel weren't exactly on a par with the kind she was used to as a model. They slapped loads of white powder all over her face and thought it was a job well done. Nikki washed it all off, did her own very simple make-up and looked more beautiful than I had ever seen her.

The hotel had found us a motor boat we could sail away in after the ceremony, and someone had put a 'Just Married' sign on the back of it. Climbing in on the beach could have been a disaster. But neither of us slipped up, though we were laughing our heads off by the time we set off. That's how everyone should leave their wedding and start married life: with tears of laughter in their eyes.

Our ready-made honeymoon was perfect too. We were strong together and we loved the number of messages hotel reception had to deal with as news got out of what we had done. Sorry to everyone who had really wanted to be at the ceremony. Thanks to everyone who said well done. Thanks, through gritted teeth, to the *News of the World* paparazzi or whoever it was who got pictures of us throughout the ceremony. We had no idea at the time – and had an even bigger shock when we saw six pages of them in *Hello!* magazine later on. We never got a penny for any of that but who cares. It was our day and in the end it was nice to share it through some good pictures.

And there was one final event that made our wedding so special. The date had been 4 March – Nikki's dad's birthday, the same day two years earlier when he had effectively given her away to me after our family meal. It couldn't have felt more perfect to have our simple ceremony on the anniversary of that gesture. And we really do believe that Brian was with us. The day after the ceremony, the hotel manager approached us holding an envelope. After watching us release our two doves the previous day, he had seen a single feather drift down from the skies on to the sand. He had picked it up and saved it for us.

A feather. The sign of an angel.

Nikki and I had already put a single white feather in every one of the post-wedding party invitations we had sent out back in London. Now we had this other feather to treasure. It meant everything. We couldn't have felt more blessed.

Back in London, Nikki and I were putting the final touches on that post-wedding celebration. We had long since decided that Zilli Fish wasn't going to be big enough, so I had gone against the first big rule in the restaurant owner's book: I had been forced to consider renting out someone else's premises.

But where? Nikki and I had decided after an afternoon out shopping in the West End. It had started to pour with rain when we got to Regent Street and we sheltered under the archway outside a place called Cocoon. We decided to take a look around and arrived, dripping, at the front desk. The staff there won us over straight away. They couldn't have been more friendly, even though we couldn't have looked less polished.

And the party itself was fantastic. Nikki persuaded me to relax about the food and let someone else take care of it. She was right. And I was glad I had someone to blame when our guests arrived. The caterers had gone for a brilliant half-Chinese, half-sushi menu. Nikki's very English family didn't exactly get fusion cuisine. My very Italian family didn't exactly understand why they were getting noodles, not pasta. Everyone looked horrified; Nikki and I thought it was hilarious.

Living with Nikki had calmed me down in every way. I kept my health kick going, becoming as obsessed by exercise and good food as I had been with drinking and late nights in my previous life. Finally, my obsessive personality was working with me, rather than against me. For years it had helped my life: my obsession with proving myself and becoming a success had done just that. Then my obsession with partying and fast living had made me lose nearly everything. Now I was on the right track. And I hope I finally understood myself enough to stay there.

Business had picked up as well. I had bought back Signor Zilli, Signor Zilli Bar, Zilli Fish and Zilli Café. I was keeping control of this tighter ship. Louisa Alves, my amazing personal assistant, was a godsend to me. Nino was still my rock. Soho itself was booming again, but more intimate restaurants were in vogue, rather than the vast soulless rooms of old. It felt good to have got things right.

The big names still agreed. Leonardo DiCaprio asked for a meal to be sent over to his studio. Mary J Blige got the same idea. She rang up asking for fish, chips and banoffee pie to be prepared for her. Her people then sent a driver to Soho to pick it up. Over in the restaurant, The Pussycat Dolls came into the kitchen and had a laughing masterclass as they helped make their own meals. David Schwimmer and Gwen Stefani sat at the same tables on consecutive nights. We started catering for private parties in hotels and big homes and met some of the capital's new super-rich residents in Belgravia and Holland Park.

Away from the restaurants, Nikki and I were also making some surprising new friends. Two of the best were Andrew Lloyd Webber and his wife Madeleine. Whenever we met up, bizarre things happened, and we soon found out that Andrew is about as different from his public image as it is possible to be. It all began a few years earlier at the magical Colony Club Hotel in Barbados. We had been having a sneaky extra holiday there and were enjoying every moment. At night, Nikki would sometimes get up and sing at dinner, joining the resident band and performing like a true professional. A couple we had been talking to one day on the beach invited us over to join them for dinner at Sandy Lane Hotel – the lady in particular thought Nikki had a wonderful voice and should sing there as well.

The following day we were on the beach when another guest came over. He too wanted to compliment Nikki on her voice. 'You're good. You know, you should meet Andrew Lloyd Webber. He's a friend of mine and he's staying on the island as well, this week,' he said.

'I'd love to meet him,' said Nikki.

'I think he's leaving soon, though,' our new friend told us.

'Well, so are we.'

'But he's flying on Concorde.'

'And so are we!' I felt fantastic pitching in with that one. Business was booming. This was the ultimate proof.

'Well, I'll tell him you'll be in the Concorde lounge.'

I'm still a bit of a nervous flier, but I was even more jumpy the next day when we headed to the airport. Sure, I'd met Hollywood royalty and real princes. But I still got butterflies about meeting some new people. And I wanted any meeting with Andrew to go well because I knew Nikki really wanted to talk to him. I knew she was a great singer. There was no one better than Andrew to advise her on making music her career.

'They're not here.' We were in the private departure lounge and felt pretty flat.

'Nikki. Over there.' Suddenly I thought I had spotted them. Two people were in the corner, hidden behind their newspapers. As the pages turned, we tried to see their faces. It was them.

'You go.' Nikki pushed me forward.

'You want to speak to him.'

'But you're the one his friend spoke to.'

'Well, you've got to be behind me.' We were like a pair of kids.

'Hello, Sir,' I began. Or should it be Lord? I should have thought about this earlier.

'Hello, Aldo.' Andrew put his paper on the table, stood up and shook my hand. I was like a kid, thrilled he knew my name. He introduced Madeleine, I introduced Nikki and we started to talk about Barbados and our holidays. 'What are you reading, Aldo?' Andrew was pointing at the book in my hand, *Kitchen Confidential*, by Anthony Bourdain.

'It's brilliant. Truer than you'd think.'

'I should read it sometime. I've forgotten to pack my book by mistake. I hate flying without something to read.'

'Well, have it. I've got another book in my bag. And I was thinking of sleeping all the way home anyway.'

As I handed over the book, the BA staff headed over to edge us gently towards the gate. We all said our goodbyes as we prepared to board the wonderful, narrow, noisy plane that was Concorde.

'We must meet for dinner back in London,' Andrew said as a final goodbye. It turned out that he meant it.

It's not easy having a meal at your own restaurant. I can't relax. I'm always wanting to jump up and help with the service, to keep things going in the kitchen, to table-hop with some other regulars. But I'd have died before taking Andrew and Madeleine to some rival restaurant. So our table for four was booked at Zilli Fish Too and once more Nikki and I were both nervous; once more, we needn't have been.

'What are we going to talk to them about?'

'How can we last a whole meal?'

'You have to make sure you get us served fast. We can't be left twiddling our thumbs waiting for the food.'

I had ordered us a big bottle of red wine to calm our nerves, but we didn't need it. Madeleine is a keen rider and knows everything about horses. My daughter had made sure I knew more than most about them as well – not least how much it costs to look after them properly. The only thing we didn't talk about was my attempt at playing polo years earlier at Ham Polo Club. It had been a disaster, and I didn't think a professional horserider like Madeleine would be impressed to hear how it had gone.

Andrew and Nikki talked about music all night. They hardly seemed to draw breath. We were like old friends from that first dinner. And just like old friends, we had a bit of a gossip.

'You know Liza Minnelli is in town? She was going to be coming over for a meal but we've not had it confirmed just yet,' I told Andrew. I had done a bit of research earlier on and found out that he had once dated her, many years ago.

'Where is she staying?'

'I don't know,' I said. 'But I can find out.'

'I'll buy you another drink if you can,' Andrew joked.

I went to the bar to make a quick call. I was desperate to get the answer so I could prove to Andrew that I had my finger on the pulse. It was my old pal Jeanette Calliva who had tipped me off. She had been hosting Liza at Chinawhite the previous night and told me that Liza was at the Lanesborough Hotel with her new husband, David Gest.

'Shall I call her?' I asked Andrew. I was showing off now, getting carried away. That big bottle of red wine had maybe been too big for a reformed drinker like me.

'Why not?' he said.

So I did. Amazingly I got straight through. Even more amazingly, Liza said she would love to see us all. So Andrew, Madeleine, Nikki and I all headed off to the Lanesborough Hotel on Hyde Park Corner, where we ordered champagne at the bar. I could tell how excited Nikki was – Liza Minnelli was one of her heroines. This was going to be quite an evening.

In the end, though, it went sour. Time passed and Liza didn't show. We called up again and, reading between the lines, I think David had put his foot down and said she should stay in their suite. We waited two full hours before heading home. Liza Minnelli had stood up Andrew Lloyd Webber. But what a night.

Next time we met up we had someone else in

common: my old pal Denise van Outen. Denise was being groomed for the role in a revived *Tell Me On A Sunday*. Nikki and I went to Andrew and Madeleine's incredible house in Sydmonton to hear Denise sing just before the official launch. She was incredible – it was as if the role had been made especially for her.

Then things got even more surreal. After lunch at Zilli Fish one day, I was talking to producer Nigel Wright about the coast and mountains of my childhood in Italy. 'You know, Andrew loves it around there. He wants to buy a house in Italy,' Nigel said.

'Well, he'll need some Italians to see him through. Nikki and I can show him around. Let's go house-hunting sometime.'

'I'll tell him.'

'And tell him it's easy to get here. Ryanair have started flying to Pescara from Stansted,' I joked.

Andrew, of course, does not do Ryanair. Or Stansted, probably. But he did want to come house-hunting. Nigel and his wife made us up to six when Andrew, Madeleine, Nikki and I flew by private plane to Italy. Did I mention it was a private plane? It was fantastic. What felt like a brand-new jet with eight huge seats and the most wonderful staff.

There was something else as well. The staff were serving my favourite food and champagne. Andrew had asked what I liked before the trip and made sure it was on board. How cool is that?

All my brothers, relatives and half of the whole Abruzzo region seemed to be crowded around the airport waiting to see this private plane land later that day. This is how I had wanted my homecoming to be all those years ago, I thought to myself. Check out my trousers this time. They're mine. They fit. Beat that! We all had some fun checking out some palazzos over the weekend, though none was exactly what Andrew and Madeleine were looking for.

On the night before our flight home, a big Italian wedding was being held at our hotel. We had all had a few glasses of wine and were relaxed and enjoying the festivities. Then Andrew decided to join in. He put a towel over his arm and started serving people drinks.

No one recognised him and I think that's why he did it. Some thought he really was their waiter. Others thought he was just a crazy Englishman. Everyone was happy. The wedding party had a pianist and a singer on the terrace and the whole night was magical. But surprisingly for Italian weddings, it seemed to wrap up early. The singer and her accompanist took their bows and left the stage; most of the guests seemed to drift away. Soon it was pretty much just the six of us left on the warm, relaxed night.

'Nikki, do you want to sing?' Andrew looked over at her.

'Now? Here?'

'Why not? They've all gone home. I'll accompany you.' And so they did. We all gave a mini round of applause as my beautiful wife joined the world's most successful composer on stage in my native Italy. This was so far beyond anything I had ever imagined.

Andrew loves playing the piano – even battered old ones in anonymous hotels. He and Nikki started off with some slow show tunes. It was beautiful. Then, something happened; someone finally got it that the man who had been playing the waiter was, in fact, Andrew Lloyd bloody Webber. I'll say one thing for us Italians: when we get enthusiastic about something, we show it. And everyone went wild for Andrew and Nikki that evening.

The whole wedding party – and more – poured back into the restaurant. Forget formality. This was Italy, and it showed. Andrew and Nikki played and sang on and off till something like 4am. I remember them taking joke bows at one stage, holding hands like little kids. Both of them were uncomfortable with applause and praise – but there are worse things to put up with.

Our fun didn't stop on the way home. We were all a bit tired as we slumped back in our big private seats for the flight. But I woke up as we zipped over the Channel. Brits are always going on about how England is being concreted over, but it still looks a green and pleasant land to me.

'Where are we?'

'That's got to be the M3.'

Nikki and I were looking out of our windows trying to spot landmarks.

'It is. That means we're near Godalming.'

I was trying to piece together the roads and the villages. Then I got it. 'Yes, that's Chris Evans's house! The big one, over there. Chris! Billie! Up here! We can see you!'

I'm sure Chris would have laughed to see how interested everyone was to spot his home – Andrew, most of all. What might have taken the smile off Chris's face was the fact that it wasn't him that Andrew was most fascinated by – it was Billie. He desperately wanted a meeting with her. 'Is she busy at the moment?' he asked me. 'Do you know what work she's doing?' Later on I heard him talking to Madeleine. 'She'd be perfect as Maria,' he said.

'I'm going to set up a dinner,' Andrew said. 'They would come over to London, wouldn't they? You and Nikki must come as well. It could be very interesting.' He was right. But not quite in the way he had expected.

Dinner with the Lloyd Webbers is a grown-up affair – even when there are kids around. When Nikki and I had been with them most recently, our fellow guests had included Sir David Frost, Glenn Close, Rowan Atkinson and his young family. These are real professionals, real celebrities, I kept thinking. This isn't a famous-for-fifteen-minutes *Big Brother* party. These people have talent. That's Mr Bean!

We expected the same for the London dinner with Chris and Billie. We made a mistake. The evening took place in the middle of Chris and Billie's party years. They were very happily married, utterly relaxed and had so much money they didn't need to worry about a thing. But would they be too relaxed for the Lloyd Webbers? I think Billie's agent could tell this could be a big deal for her and might lead to something. Everyone knew how Denise van Outen's career had leaped forward after proving herself in *Tell Me On A Sunday*. Billie could get a similar break if she played her cards right.

Nikki and I got a taxi over to Belgravia and as we climbed out we saw Chris, Billie and another man – an old friend from Portugal whom I had met a few years earlier. That night, he seemed as drunk as he was unexpected. Stranger still, he was carrying a large sports bag. Soon, this bag would produce the final big surprise of the evening.

The whole group of us then headed to Andrew's door, where we were met by his butler. A butler! I could read Nikki's mind. This was like another world. We were guided into the lift and taken up to the top floor of Andrew's incredible house. He was up there, ready to serve drinks from behind his own bar. And not just any drinks. We had Dom Perignon – thanks, Andrew. The lighting was wonderful, discreet, warm, luxurious. The surroundings matched. Mix a massive fortune with a love of art and what do you get? The Lloyd Webber home. Picture perfect. Or at least it was for a while.

Our Portuguese friend's bag spoiled things. It was moving. We found out it was Billie's birthday and Chris had bought her two puppies as a present. They were in the bag. Or at least they were till they were let out to run around the dining area and threatened to create havoc among the art works. The butler helped scoop them up on Andrew's instructions and took them downstairs, where they might do less damage – or so he hoped. Anyway, it was pretty clear that Chris and Co. had all been drinking for a while that night. Andrew soon swapped the Don Perignon for a far cheaper bottle of champagne; he clearly felt his guests were too far gone to appreciate the good stuff.

Madeleine had joined us by this point and she made a big effort to act as if this kind of thing was quite normal

– puppies and all – but I don't think she had much fun. We moved to dinner a lot sooner than Andrew's Italian chef had perhaps expected, because Andrew wasn't happy with the food.

'What do you think of this risotto?' he asked me.

'I like it,' I lied, thinking I shouldn't criticise a fellow chef.

Andrew didn't, but we left it at that. The good news was none of us had to worry about awkward silences during the meal. The bad news was that this was partly because Billie and Chris seemed to be in the middle of a row and had plenty to talk about between themselves.

'This isn't going very well, is it?' Andrew whispered to me with a bit of a smile as our plates were cleared away. But he wasn't giving up on the evening. It seemed he had a final card to play. 'So, Billie, have you ever thought of being on the West End stage?' This was the time that the rumours first surfaced that Andrew was planning a revival of *The Sound Of Music*. Our evening was something like an informal audition, and Billie could have been Maria.

'I wouldn't dream of it. You've got to be joking,' she replied.

The conversation moved on. Billie's loss became Connie Fisher's gain.

'Is there any more champagne?' our Portuguese friend asked the butler as he passed around the table clearing our final plates.

Andrew intervened, the perfect gentleman. 'I think we're all ready to leave, aren't we?' he said crushingly. A brilliant line, considering we were in his house.

So we left. But first we had to stand by as the puppies

went back in their bag. It seems neither had been house trained. I heard later that Andrew and Madeleine needed three sets of cleaning done to remove the smell from their carpets.

CHAPTER TWENTY-ONE

New Starts

I never really thought I might become a dad again at fifty. But maybe my *Fit Club* turnaround had cleaned up my whole body. Good to know everything was still in proper working order. I got the news just after I had agreed to play a bit part in an episode of *Emmerdale*.

I don't mind admitting that I was nervous up on the set in Yorkshire. Acting was another new world for me, even though I was only playing myself (as a celebrity judge in a cooking competition).

'If you can't be convincing as yourself, you've got to be the worst actor in the world,' one of my guests told me at lunch just before I headed up north for filming.

She was trying to make me feel better. But what if I didn't make a convincing Aldo Zilli? What if I really *was* the world's worst actor?!

Soap staff get a hard time in a lot of newspapers. But I knew from Michelle, Patsy and all the others just how long their hours were and how drained they could become. Up in Yorkshire, I saw first-hand how much pressure there was on the sets. Like all the other soaps, *Emmerdale* was doing far more episodes a week than in the past. The actors had to be totally professional to cope – and I didn't want to be the idiot of an amateur who ruined their days. First of all, though, I would be the idiot of an amateur whose phone went off just beside the set. Mortified, I took the message.

'Call Nikki. Urgently.'

I did.

'Aldo. I'm pregnant.'

'Nikki, I'm on the set.'

Just like my so-called marriage proposal, my Italian charm and romance deserted me. But at least I had no problem when the director called 'Action'. Until Nikki's call, I had been the most nervous man in Yorkshire. Now I was the most confident and relaxed. I was probably in shock. But, as it sank in, I became happier and happier.

I'd been desperate to start a family with Nikki. I knew she would make a wonderful mother and I was so thrilled about being a dad again. Everything, absolutely everything, felt good from that moment on. My restaurants were doing brilliantly again, I was having so much fun on television, dozens of other business opportunities were springing up. And now Nikki and I were going to have a baby. This was the fresh start I had dreamed of, the springboard to a whole new life. It was just fantastic.

Back at home, Nikki and I started a new health kick. I had learned to love clean living; Nikki loved being pregnant. It was great that so few of our friends smoked now, let alone drank. We were particularly close to Patsy Palmer – Julie, to her friends – and her husband Richard. Sitting around the table at dinner with them, there was no question of opening a bottle of wine, and I started to see why. What an insult to go to dinner with someone and effectively say you can't make it through the evening without getting drunk. What does that say about your friendship?

Towards the end of Nikki's pregnancy, I was trying to persuade her to book into somewhere swanky like the Portland Hospital for the birth. Not sure where I got that idea from, but anyway, Nikki wasn't having any of it. She wanted her baby on the NHS like everyone else. And, in the end, we couldn't beat the care we got there. Nikki first went into the Chelsea & Westminster Hospital at the end of April 2006, but we had to wait a week for our baby to arrive.

I had been coming and going throughout all of those first false alarms. But, when the doctors said we were in the final twenty-four hours, I slept on the floor so I wouldn't miss a thing. And then our baby boy was born – a week late. This meant he arrived on 4 March, the anniversary of our wedding, Nikki's dad's birthday and the day that he had quietly given her away to me the year before. It was as if our little baby had waited especially and it could hardly have been more perfect. Once more, it proved we were blessed.

Our little baby was very healthy and very loud. We decided to call him Rocco Brian Zilli. Rocco is one of the Italian saints, and we had always had fireworks in his name back in my village. Brian, of course, is in honour of Nikki's dad.

The first three months of Rocco's life weren't that calm. I was so happy that I lapsed a little from my health kick and got tempted into too many glasses of celebratory champagne. But, by the summer, reality had come home to us. A new baby was hard work. I'm sorry to say I don't remember all this from first time around with Laura. I'd not exactly been a stay-at-home dad back then, but that was what I wanted to be now. Rocco was a hyper baby – what else would you expect with parents like me and Nikki? He had his own character from the very start. A strong one.

I love my now-grown-up daughter Laura, but this time around I felt there was something different about having a son. A boy is different for a father. I felt more responsible. He will need me; he has to have someone to look up to. I wanted to take him to the football and teach him boys' things as he got older. My health kick was back. I didn't want to risk not being around. I think, like most dads, I also wanted to be the kind of man Rocco would admire and respect. I certainly didn't want to do a single thing to embarrass him. So I may have made a mistake when I agreed to be a singing chef on *Celebrity X-Factor*...

I took the call on my mobile just after lunch. It was my agent, Fiona Lindsay. She knew I was always looking for new, fun things to do – and this sounded like a cracker. The people behind the *X-Factor* were doing a celebrity show and wanted a group of singing chefs. They wanted me to be part of it. I couldn't sing a single note, but I said yes without a second thought. I called Nikki straight away. 'Nikki, guess what? I've been asked to go on the *X-Factor*. I'm going to be in a band,' I said.

'Playing an instrument?'

'No.'

'Dancing?'

'No. Singing.'

All Nikki could do was laugh.

'Laura, it's your dad. I've just agreed to go on a new version of the *X-Factor*. I'm going to be singing.'

All Laura could do was laugh as well. These are my nearest and dearest; it wasn't looking good.

I met up with my old pal Nigel Wright two days later. He was producing the show and I horrified him with my voice. Raw talent, I kept telling myself. I can be trained. I was singing alongside Jean-Christophe Novelli, Paul Rankin and my old travel mate Ross Burden. If possible, they were worse than me. What had we done?

Throughout the early rehearsals, all I could do was joke. I kept singing 'I believe I can fry', hoping that if people laughed at the lyrics they wouldn't laugh at my voice. It didn't really work. Straight away I would be reminded that being on television is nowhere near as glamorous as I'd always thought. For *Celebrity X-Factor* we were put up in a hotel in Wembley, though I managed to get home every night to be with Nikki and Rocco.

We were worked like dogs – singing dogs. We had a 7am call time every morning and often didn't get out of the studio until 2am the following day. For two weeks, the teachers and the cameras would follow us and try to kick us into shape. For two weeks, everyone laughed at us all day, every day. Our main singing coach, Yvie Burnett, deserved a medal.

Our little group attracted lots of names – Bake That was the best – and I tried to tell myself that at least the comedian in me was happy. All my life I have wanted to make people laugh; now I was doing exactly that, though I tried to forget that it wasn't in quite the way I had planned. The papers, of course, loved it. 'They sing like men in the first death throes of strangulation,' said one. And that was one of the good reviews!

Watching Simon Cowell at work alongside Sharon Osbourne and the others was another bonus of the job. He's the most businesslike man I've ever met. He tells everything like it is. And he's probably as vain as I am. I don't think I could respect him more – though I hated it when he made us take off our Bake That shirts one day.

At home, I was loving family life like never before. This time around, I loved being a dad – and I made time for it. I also just love being with Nikki. I'm still the hyperactive man who can't sit still, but somehow I love just doing nothing with my wife. I like ordinary midweek nights in; I like long weekends together. Sometimes, I turn my phone off and take days off whenever I feel like it. Rocco is completely different when I see him in the day to when I just see him at night; I want to watch him and see his moods. If I'm qualified to give any relationship advice at all, I'd say it's to spend ordinary time with the one you love. It's easy to focus on holidays or big occasions, but, if you don't take those midweek days off and do the domestic things together every now and then, do you really know each other? If you work every day, won't you just risk having a heart attack? I didn't want to retire and live with someone who had become a stranger to me. I want to be with my wife and son just as often as I can.

For all the fun of television, one thing that has kept me sane: staying close to the food. When I look back on my life, it's when I forget about my kitchens that I lose the plot. So, in the past few years, I have been looking for new ways to keep the love alive. One way has been to teach. I learned to cook though instinct, by watching my mother make the best of whatever fresh food she had on any given day. I get a buzz out of doing the same. That's why I've done London masterclasses, where small groups of us start off at the markets and look for the best of the day's deliveries. Then we use it. We don't follow rigid rulebooks. I don't shout, scream and swear if people do something a little different. And I reckon this approach gets results. I want to take the fear out of the kitchen, because that's when people really make the best food. We all laugh a lot on those teaching days too.

We took it one stage further when I helped out with a cookery school back in my old haunts in Italy. That really gave me a lift. The sunshine, the village markets, the long afternoons. A group of old friends helped with the Italian side of the organisation and I'd recommend every chef should go back to their roots every now and then. Rick Stein is the other role model for that – he's never left his roots and he's the best there is.

Anyway, after my weeks teaching in Italy, I was

itching to spruce up my menus in London. And to write a new cookbook that focuses on the way Italian families really eat.

Before then, I had a trickier challenge. The travel company Thomson had asked me to take over their in-flight catering. Everyone always jokes about airline food, but these guys wanted to do something about it. I met one of their top people, Harry Helps, and talked about the job. They had picked me because they reckoned I was the sort of person who could put people in the holiday mood. Holidays should be about enjoyment, so the food you eat on the way out shouldn't drag you down.

My kind of light, modern meals certainly make sense as in-flight food. But how can a cabin crew recreate them on board? And how can you serve them on a plastic tray in a series of smaller plastic boxes? That turned out to be the fun bit. After our first few meetings, a team of Thomson chefs came up to Zilli Fish in Soho to work on the practical stuff. I loved it. It was like a jigsaw puzzle: we had to get all the pieces right so it all fitted on the trays. Everything, right down to a single piece of cheese, has to fit. It also has to travel well. There's something about being at 35,000 feet that dulls the taste buds. So I made sure we perked things up with extra flavours.

We use a lot of sun-dried tomatoes, parmesan and chilli. We don't just use mozzarella, we use smoked mozzarella. We have gorgonzola cheeses in other dishes and we have plenty of rich Mediterranean flavours to add to the holiday mood. I also got the chance to support some of the world's best food producers back in Italy – we found some Abruzzo olive oil and we're always sourcing more natural ingredients from the region.

Put simply, I wanted to inspire people on the way out to their holidays and to keep the mood alive for a few more hours on the way home. I think we did it. If you think airline food is all rubber chicken and dry beef, then try our alternatives. We started to get good feedback straight away. People wrote and emailed to say they had never eaten so well on a plane before. Thomson is happy too. They tell me I could be serving food to around 10 million people a year now. And it's not just in the air that you can eat something Zilli. I'm opening Zilli restaurants on the company's cruise ships as well. They mainly sail around the Mediterranean in the summer and move to the Red Sea in the winter. Wherever the ships are we try to source all our food locally – including in my home region of Italy. How cool is that?

It's a hot, early summer's afternoon in 2007 and our last few lunch guests are leaving. I'm sitting at the back of the restaurant catching up on calls when I hear an old friend rush in. She's with her husband and she looks relaxed and excited. I put the phones down and take the pair to a table. It's a flying visit, but they have time for a plate of calamari and a few coffees. As they eat, I dart off to put a doggy bag together for them.

These are old friends of Nikki's and we spend a lot of weekends down with them in Brighton. When we do I always feel as if I have eaten them out of house and home. So we've developed a system: I get to stay there and eat like a pig as long as I can replenish their stocks with a load of basics every time they come to the restaurant. It's fun. Staying over with these particular friends is a clear sign of just how close we have become. I struggle to sleep in other people's houses – it doesn't matter how good the bed or how quiet the room, I feel like I'm in the way. I also end up thinking about all the times I've got to the end of an evening and told friends: 'Don't worry, of course you can stay, it's no trouble at all.' Sorry to say it, but I was always lying – I never really meant it! So I never imagine that people mean it when they say it to me. But, when we stay with these friends, I sleep like a baby. It must mean it's a genuine welcome.

In the first half of 2007, Nikki and I were spending more time down on the south coast as we thought about a move to the country. I'd not realised how much I missed the sea. I also reckon there's business to be done there. Brighton is one of my favourite towns and I'm convinced it needs a top seafood restaurant. I know it could work. Feel free to get in touch if you agree – especially if you want to help fund it. Nikki and I are always dreaming about other hare-brained schemes as well. Food businesses, restaurants, television programme ideas; we talk all night. But that's probably where we should leave it. Friendship and business can't really mix.

Nikki has taught me that it's never too late to find real happiness, and that it's worth waiting for. In 2008, I've finally got everything I've ever wanted. Restaurants that serve fantastic food to an incredible group of people.

New business challenges that come in all the time. The chance to be an entertainer on television. Most importantly, though, I've got family and friends. Those are the cornerstones of every Italian's life. And, while I've lived in England for longer than I ever lived in Italy, they're the foundation of mine.

London has changed so much since I had my first espresso at Bar Italia in Soho thirty-something years ago, but it still feels like home. It's still a place where you can make a fortune and have a lot of fun. I want to carry on doing both.

* * *

Since this book was written, someone in Brighton did get in touch and my dream of going back to the seaside has come true. Myhotels have come up with a concept and the Zilli brand will expand into Jubilee Street, Brighton, in the form of a 300 – seat resturant and café. Watch this space for the next chapter!